W9-ACA-866

THE OLD TESTAMENT
APOCRYPHA

IS VOLUME

71

OF THE

Twentieth Century Encyclopedia of Catholicism

UNDER SECTION

VI

THE WORD OF GOD

IT IS ALSO THE

120TH

VOLUME IN ORDER OF PUBLICATION

Edited by HENRI DANIEL-ROPS of the Académie Française

THE OLD TESTAMENT APOCRYPHA

By CATHERINE DIMIER

Translated from the French by S. J. TESTER

HAWTHORN BOOKS · PUBLISHERS · *New York*

 This book was manufactured in the United States of America and published simultaneously in Canada by Prentice-Hall of Canada, Ltd., 520 Ellesmere Road, Scarborough, Ontario. It was originally published in France under the title *Ce que l'Ancien Testament ne dit pas,* © Librairie Arthème Fayard, 1963. The Library of Congress has catalogued the Twentieth Century Encyclopedia of Catholicism under card number 58-14327. Library of Congress Catalogue Card Number for this volume: 64-14157. The Catholic University of America Library has catalogued this volume based on the Lynn-Peterson Alternative Classification for Catholic books: BQT184.T9v.71/BS1700. Suggested decimal classification: 229.

First edition, June, 1964

NIHIL OBSTAT

Joannes M. T. Barton, S.T.D., L.S.S.

Censor Deputatus

IMPRIMATUR

✠ Georgius L. Craven

Episcopus Sebastopolis, Vicarius Generalis

Westmonasterii, die XX APRILIS MCMLXIV

The Nihil obstat and Imprimatur are a declaration that a book or pamphlet is considered to be free from doctrinal or moral error. It is not implied that those who have granted the Nihil obstat and Imprimatur agree with the contents, opinions, or statements expressed.

ACKNOWLEDGEMENT

Permission to quote from the following work is gratefully acknowledged.
Excerpts from *The Dead Sea Scriptures in English Translation* by Theodor H. Gaster. Copyright © 1956 by Theodor H. Gaster. Reprinted by permission of Doubleday & Company, Inc.

H-9562

CONTENTS

PART II: ISRAEL'S RESISTANCE

INTRODUCTION

WHAT ARE THE OLD TESTAMENT APOCRYPHA?

There can be few more jumbled and diversified collections in literature than the Old Testament Apocrypha. It is impossible to find any common denominator in them in any field—ideas, literary forms, writers or chronology. There are among them historical books, prophetical writings, hagiography and apocalypses. Their authors were sometimes Jews—pious and nationalist Pharisees, dissident or mystical priests—sometimes naïvely apologetic Christians, and on occasion some of the host of Jewish and Christian heretics whose lucubrations in the moral and theological spheres had delayed effects over many centuries. The same confusion reigns when we come to the question of the dates when these texts were produced: if the earliest we know go back to the second century before Christ, the most recent are twelve centuries or so later.

The task of those who study these strange texts is made still more difficult by the transformations they have undergone. All the apocrypha, regarded, according to their worth and their message, with more or less esteem or suspicion, have in fact suffered from very early times a common fate: since they were unprotected by any character of sacredness, they all, with greater or less good fortune, continued on their underground way, so that many were lost, and the survival and emergence of what we have was due only to chance. They come to us often from lands far removed from the ancient Christian countries, having gone through the hands of one or more translators, who were not above making mistakes or including interpolations of their own.

Nor are we on firmer common ground when we look at the internal value of these texts. Some of them, which are animated by a truly spiritual inspiration, have at times been included among the books used for public worship, and it was only the multiplication of bizarre works, or blatantly heretical ones, which caused them to be rejected *en bloc*. The early Fathers were favourably inclined to some of them, considering them sometimes to be inspired books, and sometimes, more often, merely as edifying reading, yet on the other hand St Jerome in the fifth century treated them with the utmost rigour as the messengers of the devil and father of lies. But it must be said that the multiplication of this kind of writing and its often very mediocre quality justified this change in the course of three centuries.

So we are faced with an extraordinarily chaotic collection, through which we have no guiding thread of the normal kind: the literary form, the historical context, even the aim of the writer, are almost different for each text. The only truly common point we can find is that they all appeal to the authority of some book or person of the Old Testament, which seems to show that the writers were aware that they were producing important religious works and wanted to ensure their circulation.

But what *is* an apocryphal work? To give the word its literal Greek meaning, it is a hidden writing. The religions of antiquity offer us many examples—the Sibylline books at Rome, the annals of Egypt or Tyre, and, later, the sacred books of the mystery religions. Only the priestly caste or the initiated might read them or discuss their contents, while most people either knew nothing of them or paid them a fearful reverence. This idea of secrecy was so firmly entrenched in the minds of the peoples of antiquity that men recalled what a revolution had been the publication in the fifth century B.C.—though it was only a beginning—of the Law of the Twelve Tables, in which were promulgated the elements of

Roman Law. Another civilization, more ancient and more developed, had had its hour of glory when, about the time of Abraham, the first dynasty in Babylon made public the Code of Hammurabi. But these were extraordinary events in times when non-publication was the rule.

The Jewish mind seems to have been different from the beginning. At the moment when the Hebrew people were constituted as such, when they left Egypt and crossed the desert, about the thirteenth century B.C., God revealed his Law. It is important to notice how often the text of Scripture returns to the idea of the handing on of the whole message to everyone: "So Moses went back to the people, and told them all he was bidden" (Exod. 19. 25); "So Moses went and told the people all the Lord had said, all the commands he had given" (Exod. 24. 3); and "There I received two stone tablets, inscribed by his own divine fingers with all those commandments he gave you on the mountain, from the heart of the flames, when the people met there in full assembly" (Deut. 9. 10).

It is impossible to discover there any trace of a secret teaching, of any oral message entrusted only to a few. It was only in the first century A.D. that such an idea was entertained in the synagogue; and only in the last century that some twisted minds tried to make an Egyptian initiate out of Moses.

Later, the Holy Scriptures were deposited in the ark of the covenant and preserved in the Holy of Holies; but they were frequently copied and recopied, and were read to the faithful in their synagogues. We may notice the same spirit at work in the custom in the time of Christ of wearing fragments of the Scriptures sewn into one's clothing.

Holy Scripture itself never mentions or alludes to any other parallel teaching, and if some of the apocryphal works appeal to such teaching they rely on the authority of another apocryphal book, ancient and venerable it is true, the book of Ezra (Esdras).

But if we cannot allow that the apocryphal books were works of mystery, only for initiates, what were they?

The Greek word *apocryphos* is opposed to the word *phaneros*, which means plain, manifest, public: it is this last meaning which gives us, by opposition, the meaning of "apocrypha". Our "apocryphal" works were not for public use, they were not for public reading in places of worship, whether church or synagogue.

The Bible, of course, does not contain the whole of Hebrew literature; nor, much less, the whole of Jewish literature. We must not forget that all round the shores of the Mediterranean there flourished very important Jewish communities, at Alexandria, for example, and at Rome also, where the first persecution took place—against the Christians, it is true, but against them as a Jewish sect, and against the Jews equally. These Jewish communities in their missionary zeal produced, to aid and adapt their apostolate, spiritual and apologetic writings.

On the other hand, the Bible only covers, in its historical aspects, part of the temporal story of Israel's destiny. Its last chapters open a period of resistance of the Israelites against foreigners, Greeks first, and then Romans; but the Jews continued to write, as much to hand on the memory of what was happening as to sustain the spiritual resistance of their martyrs and exiles. Let us recall the facts.

After the Exile, Palestine was a distant and fairly contented colony of the Persian empire. Alongside the governor appointed by Susa, the Jews were in fact ruled by a High Priest appointed by themselves. Alexander in his conquest of the world skimmed lightly over Palestine which, in the division of his empire between his lieutenants that followed his death, fell to the lot of the Ptolemies. Egypt's proved a gentle enough rule, but it was quickly replaced by that of the Seleucids, who governed the East, and the desire to Hellenize the world, inherited from Alexander, had stronger and harsher effects. The interference of Antiochus IV Epiphanius

(175–163) in Palestinian affairs and the erection of a statue of Olympian Zeus in the Temple provoked resistance and persecution. This was the time of the Machabees who, in hopeless conditions, defeated the Seleucid armies. The Jews thus gained, first their religious liberty, and then, under the dynasty of the Hasmoneans, descendants of the Machabees, their political freedom. But unhappily the sons did not remain faithful to the spirit of their fathers, and the new dynasty marched swiftly down the road of Hellenization. Two parties grew up in Israel: the Pharisees, fanatical followers of the Law, and the Sadducees, who favoured compromise. Since the two factions never ceased fomenting trouble, the Romans took advantage of the situation to intervene: Pompey, after a frightful massacre, penetrated into the Temple.

There were various reactions to these upheavals. It can be seen from the story of the facts that the armed resistance of the Jews was heroic, even without hope. But alongside this, and pursuing its course further down the years, there grew an organized spiritual resistance: Israel kept alive the memory and the faith of the Covenant concluded between God and Abraham, and Israel could not die. Beyond its temporal existence and beyond the Promised Land, its unique message had to survive and be handed on. And the Jewish people had to remain faithful and holy. The finest of the Old Testament apocrypha are the reflection of this concern.

Then why are these books, some of which are magnificent and of great spiritual power, not part of Holy Scripture?

The answer is to be found in the history of the canon. An ancient tale says that after the return from exile, Ezra gathered together the holy Scriptures then existing and drew up a sort of list of recognized books. There is no basis for any such work in the Bible itself; only the fourth book of Ezra—an apocryphal book—refers to it. In the seventeenth century the exegete Richard Simon already held the tradition to be purely legendary. Nevertheless, this myth, like many others, probably enshrines some truth. At the time when Ezra and Nehemias were trying to give back to Israel, returned from exile, a keener sense of her mission, they gave the Torah a new strength and publicity. The Law, the books known as Mosaic, was in fact the basis of the Hebrew collection of the Scriptures, the other books being added to it for clarification and illustration. This is why the Samaritans, right down to our own times, only admit the books of the Law as canonical, and regard all the rest as apocryphal.

Although we cannot be precise about the details as to how it was done, all the legends and all the evidence agree that the Canon was established and closed by the second century B.C. But it is difficult to decide exactly what was the Hebrew Canon of the Scriptures.

Contemporary Hebrew Bibles, like the Protestant ones, to-day reject a certain number of books as apocryphal which the Roman Church calls deutero-canonical: Tobias, Judith, Wisdom, Ecclesiasticus, Baruch and the Second Book of Machabees. But it seems that it was not this narrower canon which was known to the first generation of Christians, for we find in their earliest writings references to books today re-jected by the Jews. One thing that is certain is that the official translation of the Jewish Bible into Greek, the Septuagint, includes the deutero-canonical books, several of which were originally written, not in Hebrew, but in Greek.

There were two attitudes of mind in Judaism in the centuries about the time of the birth of Christ. On the one hand there was the dynamic and missionary spirit of the Diaspora, having a fairly spiritualized idea of the Chosen People. On the other, there was a rigorist spirit confining itself to Palestinian Judaism, for which it was necessary to be a child of Abraham according to the flesh in order to share in the Covenant. The reaction of those who held these two views to the translation of the Bible into the vulgar tongue was symptomatic: at Alexandria, the capital of Mediterranean

Judaism, that event produced the institution of a feast of thanksgiving; but the Jewish community in Babylon, where the majority of the Palestinian Jews had taken refuge after the destruction of Jerusalem, instituted a day of reparation and of mourning for what seemed to them to be a profanation.

No doubt the primitive Church used the Scriptures in current use among those from whom she made her converts. It may be that those Judaizing Christians who gathered round St James followed the narrower Hebrew canon, but they had very little influence outside their own circle. Since the Council of Jerusalem, the outlook of St Peter himself had become more universal, and after the death of James most of the Christians who had come out of Palestinian Judaism followed the general trend, while the others formed more or less heretical Judaeo-Christian sects which scarcely survived the second century.

There can be no particularly exact treatment of the question of the canon of the Old Testament for the very early centuries of Christianity. It only became a real problem for St Jerome and the fifth century. Jerome had been asked to do a particular task: to set in order and complete the Latin translations of the Scriptures then used by Christians. What the rabbinical scholars had done to give the Greek world access to the Bible in the Septuagint version was then to be done for both Testaments: the result was what we know as the Vulgate. But with Jerome a new spirit was born: Tradition and the Spirit remained the great guides, but alongside them there were appearing textual and historical critical methods. The spirit of science took its place beside the spirit of piety.

So Jerome went back to his sources, or at least to those most accessible to him. But he had spent too long in the heart of Palestinian Judaism, which had only become more rigorous with the passage of centuries. He therefore violently rejected the "apocrypha" which had until his time been more or less admitted and tolerated in the Church; it was only obedience that brought him to translate the deutero-canonical books, or have them translated. After Jerome there were still some differences between the Roman and Greek Bibles, but gradually the usage of the Vulgate as we know it was generally imposed.

The great crisis arose with the Reformation. In his desire for purity and for a return to primitive sources, Luther adopted in a more rigorous form the positions held personally by St Jerome. The deutero-canonical books, for reasons which were more emotional than seriously critical or historical, were excluded from the corpus of the Scriptures. The Lutheran Bible adopted the canon of Palestinian Judaism. It was then the decision of the Council of Trent which finally established the canon and the Roman Bible as we have it now: the Hebrew canon plus the deutero-canonical books.

But of course it is not only for reasons based on internal or historical criticism that this book or that is admitted to be inspired while others are rejected as only "pious literature". The corpus of Holy Scriptures is not decided in the same way as the corpus of the works of Homer or Shakespeare. The Greek word *canon* had two senses: it meant a catalogue, or a rule or measure. A canonical book was thus inscribed in the catalogue of Holy Scriptures (so much for the first sense) because the Church recognized it as divinely inspired, that is, as having God for its author and as containing, with no admixture of error, the teaching revealed by God to be the rule of faith and morals (so much for the second sense). So a book was part of the canon of Scripture on the one hand if it had an ancient title to be included—the problem did not even arise, for example, in the case of the nucleus of the Old Testament, the Law or Pentateuch—or on the other hand, and this criterion was especially important for later books, if it presented a certain number of external and internal guarantees. We can see what the external guarantees were, *e contrario*, from the apocrypha. It could be asked, for example, how the Testament of Adam could have survived the Deluge to come down to our own times; or by what mysterious means part of the writings of Ezra, that great post-exilic reformer, should have been passed over in silence for several centuries. Many writings pretending to be inspired were so obviously literary forgeries that they were suspect from the beginning. The internal guarantees were more important and more delicate. The Scriptures possess an internal cohesion the elements of which become apparent precisely in proportion as they serve as a rule of a life of prayer and reflection for a community living with the presence of the Holy Spirit. Writings which do not conform to this internal cohesion but are contrary to Tradition, which is like a living Revelation, must be excluded from the canon of Scripture.

We can see, then, that however important and interesting literary and historical criticism or exegetics may be for the study of the Scriptures, the acceptance or non-acceptance of such and such a catalogue belongs in the last resort to the realm of faith. Suppose that a certain canonical work and a certain apocryphal one present exactly the same characteristics of literary form, date, authors, etc., still, if one is inscribed in the canon—canonized, in a way—the Christian must consider that one as the word of God, and not the other. All the discussions and investigations of exegetes must be carried on in the light of this. If these truths are not well understood, there is a danger that one might be unduly troubled or shocked by this or that discovery, which sheds a new light on some text or other of Scripture.

To put it quite briefly, an apocryphal book is one which is not included in the list of inspired books drawn up by the Council of Trent.

So one thing is sure: it is not doctrine which we should look for in the apocryphal books. In no case have they been considered, either by the Jews or the Church, as conveying

THE DIFFERENT CANONS OF THE SCRIPTURES

HEBREW AND PROTESTANT (PALESTINIAN)	GREEK BIBLE OF THE DIASPORA (THE SEPTUAGINT?)	CATHOLIC (TRENT)
Genesis	Genesis	Genesis
Exodus	Exodus	Exodus
Leviticus	Leviticus	Leviticus
Numbers	Numbers	Numbers
Deuteronomy	Deuteronomy	Deuteronomy
Josue	Josue	Josue
Judges	Judges	Judges
Samuel (1 & 2)	Ruth	Ruth
Kings (1 & 2)	Kings (1–4)	Kings (1–4)
Isaias	Paralipomena	Chronicles
Jeremias	Ezra (1–4)	Ezra-Nehemias
Ezechiel	Esther	Tobias
Osee, Joel, Amos,	Judith	Judith
Abdias, Jonas,	Tobias	Esther
Michaeas, Nahum,	Machabees (1–4)	Machabees (1 & 2)
Habacuc,	Psalms	Job
Sophonias,	Proverbs	Psalms
Aggaeus,	Ecclesiastes	Proverbs
Zacharias,	Song of Songs	Ecclesiastes
Malachias.	Wisdom	Song of Songs
Psalms	Ecclesiasticus	Wisdom
Job	Twelve minor	Ecclesiasticus
Proverbs	prophets: Osee,	Isaias
Ruth	Amos, Michaeas,	Jeremias
Song of Songs	Joel, Abdias,	Lamentations
Ecclesiastes	Jonas, Nahum,	Baruch
Lamentations	Habacuc,	Ezechiel
Esther	Sophonias,	Daniel
Daniel	Aggaeus,	Osee, Joel, Amos,
Ezra-Nehemias	Zacharias,	Abdias, Jonas,
Chronicles	Malachias.	Michaeas,
	Isaias	Nahum, Habacuc,
	Jeremias	Sophonias,
	Baruch 1–5	Aggaeus,
	Lamentations	Zacharias,
	Baruch 6	Malachias.
	Ezechiel	
	Daniel 13	
	Daniel 1–12	
	Daniel 14	

any message reserved for the "initiates" or the "pure"; doctrine is to be found in the canonical books, and only in them. If the apocryphal books have any real claim on our interest it can only be for other, quite different reasons.

We have already said, and it is quite obvious, that the Bible does not contain the whole of Hebrew literature. Beside the Babylonian and Egyptian cosmogonies, which were known to the Hebrews, the account of the origins of the world contained in Genesis was extraordinarily concise, for the primitive mind. The marvellous personages of Noe and the Patriarchs, as they are presented in the Old Testament, leave unsatisfied the desire for the miraculous felt by a people proud of these ancestors chosen by God in preference to all the heroes boasted of by the civilizations and religions with which they continually came in contact. It is not, then, surprising that the Israelites had their own religious folklore, and that legends and traditions formerly handed down by word of mouth should some time find their Homer to express them in literary form.

This golden legend of the Jews, of their origins, has come down to us in the apocrypha. The texts themselves are not very old; but inasmuch as Israel was a close-knit nation the need was presumably the less felt to gather together these fairy-tales, which could be handed down by oral tradition, as it were within the family. They were besides much used by Christians, who found in them good apologetic sources—when they had been mixed with a few details of a very obvious symbolism—with which to make men see more clearly the prefiguration of Christ in the history of Israel.

Still more important are those apocrypha which preserve the memory of the period which came after the time when the scriptural canon was fixed, about the fourth century B.C. The political upheavals, persecutions and corruption within the very body of the Chosen People, all seemed to many Israelites to be signs heralding the end of time. It is about this time that a curious kind of literature was born, of which the New Testament preserves a famous example: the apocalypses. An apocalypse is an account of a vision of what is going to happen in the near future. But the vision is perceived in the world "beyond", and is not expressed in ordinary human terms: sacred numbers and mysterious beasts play a great part in it. It is, as it were, a message in cipher.

Most often, it is a literature of vengeance. The unclean beast is Rome, surrounded by a terrifying menagerie representing the emperor's lackeys, Israelite governors and kings whose habits and inclinations led them to go over to the invader. Rome might triumph for a time, but the Lord would have the last word, and he reserved glory and blessedness for his Chosen People. No longer is there any call to armed resistance, but the general spirit of these apocalypses is still centred on the re-establishment of the earthly power of Israel. The Jews did not place their hopes in man, but in the Lord God of Hosts.

An entirely different kind of writing dates from the same period. Many Jews, faced by the disasters which shook their nation, felt the need for conversion, for a return to the God who demanded a contrite and humble heart. The apocrypha offer us precious evidence of this spiritual reaction. The Essenes were related to this movement within Judaism; they retired from the world to live purely before the Lord. Recent discoveries in the caves at Qumran have now enabled us to know them better, as well as furnishing us with texts before unknown.

All these works, in their different degrees, present us with a common interest: they are part, one might say, of the moral ground of revelation. Nothing that affects our knowledge of the people God chose for himself can be indifferent in our eyes. Now God, himself made flesh, did not reveal his message abstractly or in a form without body. God's people, like their neighbours, had known a primitive age, and a history happy at one time and unhappy at others. In a certain way, the apocrypha belong to biblical archaeology. But like cities which are revealed little by little under the excavator's spade, cities wherein are mingled coins and pottery and stones of different periods, the para-biblical books have been carried down to us on the waters of very various rivers. Every day new discoveries make us question the discoveries of yesterday. This has become more than ever true in the last ten years: the manuscripts in the Dead Sea scrolls have not all been published yet, nor even properly listed.

However, there are texts, texts which nourished the piety of the early Christians—for some of them found their place in the first Bibles—and there are legends in them which still live on the portals of cathedrals, taken up into our history.

We cannot examine them all. We have only fragments of many of them, and their origins are more than doubtful. Even to try and give a complete list would be as tiresome as it is impossible. Only think, for example, that the most recent date from the tenth century A.D., and that separatists and heretics of the three religions which confess the authority of the Bible—Judaism, Christianity and Islam—have made up large numbers of revelations and stories fathered on to the saints of the Old Testament.

Through the finest of these apocrypha we shall try to listen to Israel singing or weeping or praying, to hear the preaching of the most artless of the first Christians.

Alongside the splendours of the liturgy, the Church allows piety to express itself in songs which are simple and charming, and sometimes very beautiful. Should we not allow room, beside the revealed Word of God, for these canticles, the apocrypha?

I shall now give a list, with brief notes, of the most important apocrypha of the Old Testament. It seemed better to give in the body of this book only a few long extracts, to show the general lines of this pseudepigraphic literature, which are more pleasant to read than a large number of shorter passages which must inevitably often repeat the same thing, though taken from different books.

The passages chosen for quotation have been selected for their clear meaning, their narrative interest or their emotional significance. I have tried to reproduce the Jewish climate in these centuries about the birth of Christ, rather than to extract the necessarily scattered and sometimes very obscure historical or doctrinal information which makes the apocrypha important sources for the study of the Old and New Testaments.

THE MOST IMPORTANT OLD TESTAMENT APOCRYPHA

The Book of Jubilees, or *The Little Genesis*

Written before the second century A.D. by a pious Jew, this is a history of the people of God from the beginnings to the Exodus, as revealed to Moses by an angel. Some fragments of it have been found among the Dead Sea scrolls. Through this story, divided into fifty "jubilees" of forty-nine years, the writer wished to encourage those Jews who observed the Law, and to stigmatize those who allowed themselves to be corrupted by Hellenistic ways. The observances of the Law were revalued: the Sabbath became more important, and so on, each change being given some authority by making it go back to the origins of mankind. (See Chapter IV of this book.)

3 Machabees

This is quoted almost in full in Chapter III.

3 Ezra (or *1 Esdras* in Charles)

Written in the first century B.C. by an Alexandrian Greek, this is a patchwork of passages from the Bible relating to the history of the Temple. Its influence was so great during the early centuries of the Church that it was included in the ancient editions of the Vulgate.

The Books of Adam and Eve

These are a whole collection of books concerned with Adam and Eve and their children. They include a curious heretical work, *The Book of Adam*; the *Testament of Adam*, the *Book of the Daughters of Adam*, the *Conflict of Adam*, the *Penitence of Adam*, and so on, in which are gathered the eastern legends of the earthly paradise, our first parents and their children. (See Chapters I and II.)

The Testaments of the XII Patriarchs

This is a Jewish work of the end of the second century B.C. The twelve sons of Jacob, on their deathbeds, give their last instructions to their children. Each patriarch is a sort of pattern of a vice to avoid or a virtue to practise; the book is a long, romanticized moral treatise.

The Psalms of Solomon

They were written in the first century B.C. by one or more Palestinian Jews, contemporaries of the capture of Jerusalem and the profanation of the Temple by Pompey. They are very close to the Psalms in their form and spirit, and express the best aspects of the Jewish mind, in its faith and hope in Yahweh, its patriotism and messianic hopes. (See Chapter IV.)

4 Machabees

What we have here is a typical "discourse" of a Hellenistic Jew of the first century A.D. The martyr Eleazar and his seven children serve as a demonstration of the Stoic thesis of the sovereign mastery of the reason over the passions.

The Book of Enoch, or *1 Enoch*, or *The Ethiopian Enoch*

All these titles refer to the same book, the finest and richest of the surviving apocrypha of the Old Testament. It is also the book which enjoyed the greatest authority among the Jews and the first Christians. Although it was written in Hebrew, it is a compilation of a number of works dating from the second half of the second and the first half of the first century B.C. The whole of it has only been preserved in an Ethiopian version. With its eyes on the Last Judgement, it is a history of the origin of the world, of the fall of the angels, of the part played by the angels in the working of the world, and of the succession of kingdoms until the coming of the Messias. (See Chapter I.)

The Book of the Secrets of Enoch (*2 Enoch* in Charles)

This book, which has come down to us in two Slavonic versions, one of which is clearly an abridgement of the other, is apparently the work of an Alexandrian Jew of the first century. Enoch is taken up into heaven, where he successively visits all seven heavens. He receives revelations concerning the creation of the world and the fall of our first parents, and then after a short interval on earth when he recounts his visions he is once again taken up into heaven.

The Assumption of Moses

Written by a rigid and nationalist Pharisee in the first century A.D., this book is presented as the testament of Moses to his descendants. It is the story of Israel from Josue to the death of Herod. The book ends with the future apotheosis of the Jewish people, for whom the world was made, and who, after they have suffered punishment for their crimes, shall rule the universe.

4 Ezra

The work of a Jew at the end of the first century A.D., it recounts the seven visions of Ezra, relating to the end of the world and the Last Judgement. Problems of the destiny of the individual, of salvation, and of the intercession of the saints are here posed in a very moving way. (See Chapter IV.)

Apocalypse of Abraham

This Jewish work of the first century A.D. recounts the story of the conversion of Abraham.

Apocalypse of Baruch (*3 Baruch* in Charles)

Similar to and contemporary with 4 Ezra, it is a history of the miseries of Israel, which are to be followed by the brilliant reign of the Messias. To prepare for its coming, Jewish sinners must be converted and observe the Law.

The Dead Sea Scrolls (See Chapter V)

The most important for our purposes are:

The Manual of Discipline
The Zadokite Document
The Commentary on the Book of Habakkuk
The War of the Sons of Light and the Sons of Darkness

PART I

THE GOLDEN LEGEND OF THE OLD TESTAMENT

CHAPTER I

ANGELOLOGY, COSMOGONY AND PHYSICS

If we consider the various civilizations with which Israel was in more or less close contact—relations of neighbourliness at times of independence or conquest, relations of master and slave in times of captivity or foreign domination—one thing is immediately obvious: the essential problems of the origin of the world, of the place of man in the universe, and of the relationship between man and God were all conceived in an absolutely original way by the Jews.

Look at the Scriptures: the story of the creation of the world, apart from man, takes up only one chapter of Genesis, and that is concerned only with the visible world, that which is immediately perceptible by all. The great business of the creation is with man—with man, created by God male and female, and in direct communication with God. The Bible is essentially the story of the relations of man with God, and it has little to say about the angels.

Now let us briefly glance at the treatment accorded to these subjects among the Egyptians, the Babylonians and the Greeks, the peoples with whom the Jews were in contact throughout their history.

How were they dealt with at the time when the apocrypha were produced? To begin with, the first creative principle was ill defined. Creation is most often a series of degradations of the first principle, to the point at which it is more or less explicitly destroyed by its very creatures; hence the frightful struggles among the gods in which one devours his father while another eats his own children, and the constant opposition of the male principle (the first principle) to the female (the principle of reproduction, and hence of degradation), so that when we come to man, we are very far from the spirit of the first God, and if man is still a pale reflection of God, it is almost accidentally and, in any case, by a peculiar bastardization.

Another almost general characteristic of the most ancient cosmogonies, though often not explicit, is the assimilation of matter and evil. One of the first generations of the first principle is an evil god; and it is from him that matter comes, the sensible world, the body of man. So the human being, far from being a whole imagined and created by a personal and intelligent God as master of the visible world (Gen. 2. 7; 19–21), is an unfortunate and fortuitous coming together of a material principle (which is in itself evil) and an emanation from a far-removed first spirit. Man is not a unity: he is a being essentially torn in two. He has no direct relationship with the divinity, but at most a possibility of coming into contact with intermediate spirits.

Such doctrines must necessarily have produced magic, ways of approaching those spirits, and metempsychosis, which is a method of climbing back up the ladder of being; and dualism, which produced crowds of "the pure" or "initiates" careful to separate themselves from the common herd and to free themselves from the tragic lot of the rest of men.

When we remember that the Chosen People lived surrounded by peoples with this outlook and these beliefs, we can the better understand the fanatical zealousness of Israel's leaders in preserving their people by every means from contamination.

At the time when the apocrypha were being produced, the thought of Israel was up against the Hellenistic world, and in particular Platonism, in which those beliefs had received their most seductive and most rational expression and explanation. How could the story of Genesis not appear to cultivated minds, especially to Hellenized Jews, a bit shallow, a bit earthy? Had not the problems which at that time passionately involved the minds and hearts of men been conjured out of existence?

But if, as we have just said, the cosmogony of Genesis was extremely concise, what are we to say of angelology?

It is true that the devil, the spirit of evil, is represented by the serpent, but he is not shown to us as the spirit of evil, but as one of "the beasts which the Lord had made", and "there was none that could match him in cunning" (Gen. 3. 1). It is only when the man and the woman are banished from Eden that the Cherubim appear (Gen. 3. 24), celestial spirits, and servants of God. Both are, if not supernumeraries, at least very minor actors. Still the drama is played out between man and God.

Nor is there any trace of that outlook which entrusted the running of the world to celestial spirits: it is Adam who names all creatures (Gen. 2. 19–21), which is to say, submits them to his sway, and that by the command of God himself.

Now was not all this too short, too simple, for the profoundly intellectualized world of Hellenism? Part of the apocryphal literature seems to have been intended, not to fill in the gaps in Genesis—the first and the best of the writers of these books, as we have already said, laid no claim to be imparting any teaching other than what was in the Book—but in a way to build bridges across the gulf which separated the religion of Israel from the philosophic or religious outlook of those who surround it.

There are many passages which deal with celestial spirits. I shall restrict my quotations to those which treat questions of importance: the struggle between the good and evil angels, the order of celestial spirits, the lot of the fallen angels and the struggle between demons and men.

This is how the *Book of the Conflict of Adam* describes the combat of the good and evil spirits (an angel is talking to Adam):

> We know what Satan did concerning the angels before he was cast from heaven. He gathered together his company and deceived them and promised them that he would give to them divinity and a great kingdom, and made to them all the promises which he has made to thee in like manner. And his company believed that his word was true and rebelled against God. And he sent to us that we should submit to his orders and should obey his commands, but we would not, but rejected his counsel. And after he had fought with God and had insulted his divine majesty, he gathered together his followers and fought against us. But the strength of God was with us, and without that strength we should not have mastered him; we cast him down from the height of heaven to the lowest place, and his fall was the cause of great joy in heaven. Had he remained in heaven, no angel would have remained there; but in his mercy God drove him far from us and sent him down to dwell in darkness.

After the separation of the good from the evil, the celestial spirits were divided according to their greatness and their functions. I quote again from the *Book of the Conflict of Adam*, and notice the influence of Platonism and Stoic doctrine: the lowest office, entrusted to the lowest order of angels, is that of guarding men, the other orders presiding over the working of the world. We notice also the reference to the belief in a "guardian angel" appointed for each man, which is nowhere explicitly mentioned in the Scriptures.[1]

[1] The guardian angels are certainly implicit in what our Lord says about the "little ones" in Matt. 18. 10.

The lowest order is that of the Angels, and the task which has been entrusted to them by God is to watch over each man. To every man living in this world is allotted as his guardian an angel of this lowest order, and this is his office.

The second order is that of the Archangels, and their task is to make all things to live according to the order of God's ordering. All that exists in creation, animals of the earth, or winged animals, or reptiles, or fishes of the sea, all creatures that are in the world save man alone are entrusted to their care and government.

The third order is that of the Principalities, and their task is to hie themselves to the places where the clouds rise from the ends of the earth, according to the word of David, and to cause the rain to descend from thence upon the earth. All the changes in the air, rain and hail and snow and dust-storms and showers of blood are all produced by them, and to them also belong the storm-clouds and the lightning.

The fourth order is that of the Powers, and their task is the government of all light-giving bodies, such as the sun and the moon and the stars.

The fifth order is that of the Virtues, and their task is to prevent the demons from destroying the creation of God for envy of man. For if it were allowed to the accursed race of demons to do their own will for one hour, then on the instant they would overturn the whole of creation; if, I say, the power of God did not keep watch over them and had not imposed upon them guardians who should prevent them from doing the evil that they will.

The sixth order is that of the Dominations, and their task is to have the oversight of all kingdoms. In their hands are victory and defeat, as the king of Assyria shewed: when he marched against Jerusalem, an angel descended and struck and scattered his wicked host, and in an instant he lost a hundred and eighty thousand men. Holy Zacharias also saw an angel like unto a man riding on a red bay mare standing in the shade of a grove of trees, and behind him white and red horses ridden by angels with swords drawn in their hands. Judas Machabaeus also saw an angel riding on a red horse, holding in his hand a golden cup; and when the army of Antiochus the unholy perceived that angel, they took flight before his face. All victories and all defeats, these are they who decide them according to the sign of God who has entrusted to them the overseeing of war.

The other orders are those of the Thrones, the Seraphim and the Cherubim. These are they who stand before the greatness of the Lord and serve his throne and continually at all times make him offerings and worship him. The Cherubim with all reverence hold up the throne and the seal of God is in their hands. The Seraphim wait upon our Lord. The Thrones stand at the door of the Holy of Holies.

Such are in truth the divisions of the tasks entrusted to the angels who have the government of this world.

Two other questions are closely connected with this: the fate of the fallen angels—harsher than that of man, for they have no possibility of redemption—and the hatred which the spirit of evil feels towards Adam and towards all mankind precisely because for them redemption is possible, and because they have usurped his place as master of the earth. This is how the *Book of Enoch* describes to us the fate of the fallen angels:

Judgement has been pronounced against you, and useless are all your prayers.

So henceforth you shall no longer go up into heaven, and on earth you shall dwell in chains as long as the earth itself shall endure.

But first shall you witness the ruin of all that is dear to you; no longer shall you possess them, they shall fall by the sword before your very eyes.

Pray no more, neither for them nor for yourselves.

But you shall weep, and in silence shall your supplication be made.

Never shall you obtain mercy, never shall peace be given unto you.

Satan, in the book called *The Penitence of Adam*, directly attacks man:

God made a covenant with Adam to rescue him from all the disasters into which he fell; no covenant did he make with me, and from my troubles he will not deliver me. And to Adam and his posterity he promised that he would allow them to dwell in the land where I was. I shall slay Adam, so that the earth is relieved of his presence and will remain wholly mine; if he is slain, he will have no posterity to inherit the heavenly kingdom, and my kingdom will be left for me, and God will have to call me, me and my company, back into my kingdom.

But because the original fall was not great enough to kill Adam and his race for ever, the spirit of evil must continue the fight at the head of his forces; his lieutenants have to fulfil particular tasks in order to corrupt the descendants of the first man past hope of redemption:

And Azazel taught men to make swords, and knives, and shields, and breastplates, and made known to them the metals ⟨of the earth⟩ and the art of working them, and bracelets and ornaments, and the use of antimony, and the beautifying of the eyelids, and all kinds of costly stones, and all colouring tinctures.[2]

And there arose much godlessness, and they committed fornication, and they were led astray, and became corrupt in all their ways.

Semjâzâ taught enchantments, and root-cuttings, 'Armârôs the resolving of enchantments, Barâqîjâl ⟨taught⟩ astrology, Kôkabêl the constellations, Êzêqêêl the knowledge of the clouds ⟨Araqiêl the signs of the earth, Shamsiêl the signs of the sun⟩, and Sariêl the course of the moon.[3]

Another curious aspect of the relations between men and angels, of which some traces are to be found in the Bible, and which made up an important chapter of ancient mythologies,

[2] Notice in this passage the Mazdaist interpretation of matter and of working in and with matter.

[3] *The Book of Enoch*; translated by R. H. Charles, in Charles, *The Apocrypha and Pseudepigrapha of the Old Testament in English*, vol. II, p. 192.

was the story of the giants. All ancient civilizations preserved a memory of this extraordinary race of supermen; Titans or Giants were either the predecessors or the enemies of the first men. In certain mythologies, they are one of the levels of transformation of the first spirit in its downward evolution, and engage in an open fight with that spirit. In others, they are the product of the union of spirits with the daughters of men.

The Bible mentions them in several places, but without saying much about them. They are shown as having lived before the Deluge (Gen. 6. 4; Wis. 14. 6), and as being the fruit of the union of the sons of God with the daughters of men (Gen. 6. 4), but the writer of the sacred text tries to fit them into a kind of historical context, half rationalizing them —"these were the heroes whose fame has come down to us from long ago."

The existence and the problem of the giants is treated in several places in the apocrypha. It is noticeable that even when these writers consider the giants as coming before the creation of the world, they never make them beings who could rival God or cause him any harm. Here too, whatever contamination was suffered either intellectually or spiritually because of neighbouring civilizations, the essential ideas of God as creator and transcendent are fully safeguarded.

Here first is a passage from the *Book of Enoch* in which the existence of giants is attributed to unions between angels and women:

> And it came to pass when the children of men had multiplied that in those days were born unto them beautiful and comely daughters. And the angels, the children of the heaven, saw and lusted after them, and said to one another: "Come, let us choose us wives from among the children of men and beget us children." And Semjâzâ, who was their leader, said unto them: "I fear ye will not indeed agree to do this deed, and I alone shall have to pay the penalty of a great sin." And they

all answered him and said: "Let us all swear an oath, and all bind ourselves by mutual imprecations not to abandon this plan but to do this thing." Then sware they all together and bound themselves by mutual imprecations upon it.... And all the others together with them took unto themselves wives, and each chose for himself one, and they began to go in unto them and to defile themselves with them, and they taught them charms and enchantments, and the cutting of roots, and made them acquainted with plants. And they became pregnant, and they bare great giants, whose height was three thousand ells: who consumed all the acquisitions of men. And when men could no longer sustain them, the giants turned against them and devoured mankind. And they began to sin against birds and beasts and reptiles and fish, and to devour one another's flesh, and drink the blood.[4]

Other, somewhat later apocrypha cannot admit the principle of the possibility of such unions between immaterial spirits and humankind. Having shown that they are unlikely and impossible, they take up the story as it is told in Genesis, in greater detail, and provide it with a sort of historical explanation:

And Noe preached often amongst the children of Cain; but the children of Seth who had come down from the holy mountain dwelt then amongst the children of Cain, and were soiled with their impurity and bare children among them, and their children were called *ganani*, that is, giants, who were men of great strength and huge stature, and they had no equals. Now of them ancient wise men have written that the angels came down from the heaven and associated themselves with the daughters of Cain, and that from them they engendered the giants. But in this opinion they were mistaken and it is not true that angels, who are pure spirits, could mingle in sin with men. If indeed that had been possible to them, there would not be left one unsullied woman on the earth, for the Satans are wicked and perverse. But according to their being and their nature, they are neither male nor female, but pure spirits, who

[4] Trans. R. H. Charles, in Charles, vol. II, pp. 191–2.

since their fall have become spirits of darkness. And there are many who say that the angels who had fallen from the heaven had associated with women and borne children, but this cannot be true: they were truly children of Adam who had dwelt long on the holy mountain, and as long as they retained their virginity and their purity and their superiority, as the angels retained theirs, they were called angels of God. But when they had violated the commandments of God and had associated themselves with the children of Cain and had engendered children, ignorant people said that angels had descended from the heaven and had associated themselves with the daughters of men and had engendered the giants.

Now every ancient philosophy includes some "physics": that is, a part of philosophy concerned with the knowledge of nature. In the Hellenistic period, with the interpenetration of cultures in the Mediterranean world and with the predominant influence of Platonism, which had taken on more and more the value of religion, this "physics" was no longer basically scientific philosophical thinking, as it had been in the time of Aristotle. It had taken on a strongly "mysterious" character. Astrology and symbolic playing with numbers were closely mixed with rigorously scrupulous observation.

Now, there is no trace of this physics in the Bible. The physical phenomena which are described are those of a miraculous character, while this character belongs more to the circumstances in which they occur than to the phenomena themselves. Take as an example the passage of the Red Sea, or the manna, both from Exodus. Natural explanations have been put forward. But what do they matter? The storyteller gives no long and detailed physical description of these marvels, nor does he lay any stress on the material character of either phenomenon. What is important about each is that it was produced at exactly that precise moment when it was vital for the people of God that they should take place. Here as before, it is the men who are at the heart of the matter, and the unfolding of the saving plan of God for his people.

The apocryphal writers, on the other hand, wanted to put forward a description and explanation of natural phenomena.

The most remarkable passages, from this point of view, occur in the *Book of Enoch*. It will be best to quote them *in extenso*, because it is particularly on this subject that can best be seen the concern at the heart of the best of the apocrypha to preserve what is essential in Judaism while remaining alive to the world about them.

First, I quote a vision and an explanation of atmospheric phenomena:

> And the other angels who went with me and showed me what was hidden told me what is first and last in the heaven in the height, and beneath the earth in the depth, and at the ends of the heaven, and on the foundation of the heaven. And the chambers of the winds, and how the winds are divided, and how they are weighed, and ⟨how⟩ the portals of the winds are reckoned, each according to the power of the wind, and the power of the lights of the moon, and according to the power that is fitting: and the divisions of the stars according to their names, and how all the divisions are divided. And the thunders according to the places where they fall, and all the divisions that are made among the lightnings that it may lighten, and their host that they may at once obey. For . . . the thunder and lightning are inseparable, and although not one and undivided, they both go together through the spirit and separate not. For when the lightning lightens, the thunder utters its voice, and the spirit enforces a pause during the peal, and divides equally between them; for the treasury of their peals is like the sand, and each one of them as it peals is held in with a bridle, and turned back by the power of the spirit, and pushed forward according to the many quarters of the earth. And the spirit of the sea is masculine and strong, and according to the might of his strength he draws it back with a rein, and in like manner it is driven forward and disperses amid all the mountains of the earth. And the spirit of the hoar-frost is his own angel, and the spirit of the hail is a good angel. And the spirit of the snow

has forsaken his chambers on account of his strength—there is a special spirit therein, and that which ascends from it is like smoke, and its name is frost. And the spirit of the mist is not united with them in their chambers, but it has a special chamber; for its course is glorious both in light and in darkness, and in winter and in summer, and in its chamber is an angel. And the spirit of the dew has its dwelling at the ends of the heaven, and is connected with the chambers of the rain, and its course is in winter and summer: and its clouds and the clouds of the mist are connected, and the one gives to the other. And when the spirit of the rain goes forth from its chamber, the angels come and open the chamber and lead it out, and when it is diffused over the whole earth it unites with the water on the earth.... For the waters are for those who dwell on the earth; for they are nourishment for the earth from the Most High who is in heaven: therefore there is a measure for the rain, and the angels take it in charge.

Even more perhaps than by the observation of meteorological phenomena, antiquity was fascinated by and deeply interested in the succession of day and night, the seasons and the years. "The two great luminaries" of Genesis, created to command the day and the night, seemed extraordinary and quasi-divine to the ancients. The east was divided between religions of the sun and religions of the moon. Astronomy and astrology go back to the earliest times. As early as the time of Moses, the Israelites had to be warned against worshipping the sun or the moon. As the science of observation improved, how could men not be struck by the regularities of the stars, governed, it seemed, by a mathematical intelligence?

I have thought it worth while to quote the following passage from the *Book of Enoch* in its entirety, despite its repetitions and obscurities. The dividing line between minute observation and symbolic interpretation is constantly and, as it were, unconsciously crossed; the sun and the moon are creatures, it is true—but are they material creatures?

The book of the courses of the luminaries of the heaven, the relations of each, according to their classes, their dominion and their seasons, according to their names and places of origin, and according to their months, which Uriel, the holy angel, who was with me, who is their guide, showed me; and he showed me all their laws exactly as they are, and how it is with regard to all the years of the world and unto eternity, till the new creation is accomplished which dureth till eternity. And this is the first law of the luminaries: the luminary the sun has its rising in the eastern portals of the heaven, and its setting in the western portals of the heaven. And I saw six portals in which the sun rises, and six portals in which the sun sets: and the moon rises and sets in these portals, and the leaders of the stars and those whom they lead: six in the east and six in the west, and all following each other in accurately corresponding order: also many windows to the right and left of these portals. And first there goes forth the great luminary, named the Sun, and his circumference is like the circumference of the heaven, and he is quite filled with illuminating and heating fire. The chariot on which he ascends, the wind drives, and the sun goes down from the heaven and returns through the north in order to reach the east, and is so guided that he comes to the appropriate (lit. "that") portal and shines in the face of the heaven. In this way he rises in the first month in the great portal, which is the fourth [those six portals in the east]. And in that fourth portal from which the sun rises in the first month are twelve window-openings, from which proceed a flame when they are opened in their season. When the sun rises in the heaven, he comes forth through that fourth portal thirty mornings in succession, and sets accurately in the fourth portal in the west of the heaven. And during this period the day becomes daily longer and the night nightly shorter to the thirtieth morning. On that day the day is longer than the night by a ninth part, and the day amounts exactly to ten parts and the night to eight parts. And the sun rises from that fourth portal, and sets in the fourth and returns to the fifth portal of the east thirty mornings, and rises from it and sets in the fifth portal. And then the day becomes longer by two parts and amounts to eleven parts, and the night becomes shorter and amounts to seven parts. And it returns to the east and enters into the sixth portal, and rises and sets in the sixth portal one-and-thirty mornings on account of its sign. On that day the day becomes longer than the night, and the day becomes double the night, and the day becomes twelve parts, and the night is shortened and becomes six parts. And the sun mounts up to make the day shorter and the night longer, and the sun returns to the east and enters into the sixth portal and rises from it and sets thirty mornings. And when the thirty mornings are accomplished, the day decreases by exactly one part, and becomes eleven parts, and the night seven. And the sun goes forth from that sixth portal in the west, and goes to the east and rises in the fifth portal for thirty mornings, and sets in the west again in the fifth western portal. On that day the day decreases by two parts, and amounts to ten parts, and the night to eight parts. And the sun goes forth from that fifth portal and sets in the fifth portal of the west, and rises in the fourth portal for one-and-thirty mornings on account of its sign, and sets in the west. On that day the day is equalized with the night, [and becomes of equal length], and the night amounts to nine parts and the day to nine parts. And the sun rises from that portal and sets in the west, and returns to the east and rises thirty mornings in the third portal and sets in the west in the third portal. And on that day the night becomes longer than the day, and night becomes longer than night, and day shorter than day till the thirtieth morning, and the night amounts exactly to ten parts and the day to eight parts. And the sun rises from that third portal and sets in the third portal in the west and returns to the east, and for thirty mornings rises in the second portal in the east, and in like manner sets in the second portal in the west of the heaven. And on that day the night amounts to eleven parts and the day to seven parts. And the sun rises on that day from the second portal and sets in the west in the second portal, and returns to the east into the first portal for one-and-thirty mornings, and sets in the first portal in the west of the heaven. And on that day the night becomes longer and amounts to the double of the day: and the night amounts exactly to twelve parts and the day to six. And the sun has therewith traversed the divisions of his orbit and turns again on those divisions of his orbit, and enters that portal thirty mornings and sets also in the west opposite to it. And on that night has the night decreased in length by a ninth part, and the night has become eleven parts and the day seven parts. And the sun has returned and entered into the second portal in the east, and returns on those divisions of his orbit for thirty mornings, rising and setting. And on that day the night decreases in length, and the night amounts to ten parts and the day to eight. And on that day the sun rises from that portal, and sets in the west, and returns to the east, and rises in the third portal for one-and-thirty mornings, and sets in the west of the heaven. On that day the night decreases and amounts to nine parts, and the day to nine parts, and the night is equal to the day and the year is exactly as to its days three hundred and sixty-four. And the length of the day and of the night, and the shortness of the day and of the night arise—through the course of the sun these distinctions are made (lit. "they are separated"). So it comes that its course becomes daily longer, and its course nightly shorter. And this is the law and the course of the sun, and his return as often as he returns sixty times and rises, i.e. the great luminary which is named the sun, for ever and ever. And that which thus rises is the great luminary, and is so named according to its appearance, according as the Lord commanded. As he rises, so he sets and decreases not, and rests not, but runs day and night, and his light is sevenfold brighter than that of the moon; but as regards size they are both equal.

And after this law I saw another law dealing with the smaller luminary, which is named the Moon. And her circumference is like the circumference of the heaven, and her chariot in which she rides is driven by the wind, and light is given to her in ⟨definite⟩ measure. And her rising and setting change every month: and her days are like the days of the sun, and when her light is uniform (i.e. full) it amounts to the seventh part of the light of the sun. And thus she rises. And her first phase in the east comes forth on the thirtieth morning: and on that day she becomes visible, and constitutes for you the first phase of the moon on the thirtieth day together with the sun in the portal where the sun rises. And the one half of her goes forth by a seventh part, and her whole circumference is empty, without light, with the exception of one seventh part of it, ⟨and⟩ the fourteenth part of her light. And when she receives one seventh part of the half of her light, her light amounts to one seventh part and the half thereof. And she sets with the sun, and when the sun rises the moon rises with him and receives the half of one part of light, and in that night in the beginning of her morning [in the commencement of the lunar day] the moon sets with the sun, and is invisible that night with the fourteen parts and the half of one of them. And she rises on that day with exactly a seventh part, and comes forth and recedes from the rising of the sun, and in her remaining days she becomes bright in the ⟨remaining⟩ thirteen parts.

And I saw another course, a law for her, ⟨and⟩ how according to that law she performs her monthly revolution. And all these Uriel, the holy angel who is leader of them all, showed to me, and their positions, and I wrote down their positions as he showed them to me, and I wrote down their months as they were, and the appearance of their lights till fifteen days were accomplished. In single seventh parts she accomplishes all her light in the east, and in single seventh parts accomplishes all her darkness in the west. And in certain months she alters her settings, and in certain months she pursues her own peculiar course. In two months the moon sets with the sun: in those two middle portals the third and the fourth. She goes forth for seven days, and turns about and returns again through the portal where the sun rises, and accomplishes all her light: and she recedes from the sun, and in eight days enters the sixth portal from which the sun goes forth. And when the sun goes forth from the fourth portal she goes forth seven days, until she goes forth from the fifth and turns back again in seven days into the fourth portal and accomplishes all her light: and she recedes and enters into the first portal in eight days. And she returns again in seven days into the fourth portal from which the sun goes forth. Thus I saw their position—how the moons rose and the sun set in those days. And if five years are added together the sun has an overplus of thirty days, and all the days which accrue to it for one of those five years, when they are full, amount to 364 days. And the overplus of the sun and of the stars amounts to six days: in 5 years 6 days every year come to 30 days: and the moon falls behind the sun and the stars to the number of 30 days. And the sun and the stars bring in all the years exactly, so that they do not advance or delay their position by a single day unto eternity; but complete the years with perfect justice in 364 days. In 3 years there are 1,092 days, and in 5 years 1,820 days, so that in 8 years there are 2,912 days. For the moon alone the days amount in 3 years to 1,062 days, and in 5 years she falls 50 days behind: [i.e. to the sum ⟨of 1,770⟩ there is to be added ⟨1,000 and⟩ 62 days.] And in 5 years there are 1,770 days, so that for the moon the days in 8 years amount to 2,832 days. All the days she falls behind in 8 years are 80. And the year is accurately completed in conformity with their world-stations and the stations of the sun, which rise from the portals through which it (the sun) rises and sets 30 days.

And the leaders of the heads of the thousands, who are placed over the whole creation and over all the stars, have also to do with the four intercalary days, being inseparable from their office, according to the reckoning of the year, and these render service on the four days which are not reckoned in the reckoning of the year. And owing to them men go wrong therein, for those luminaries truly render service on the world-stations, one in the first portal, one in the third portal of the heaven, one in the fourth portal, and one in the sixth portal, and the exactness of the year is accomplished through its separate three hundred and sixty-four stations. For the signs and the times and the years and the days the angel Uriel showed to me, whom the Lord of glory hath set for ever over all the luminaries of the heaven, in the heaven and in the world, that they should rule on the face of the heaven and be seen on the earth, and be leaders for the day and the night, i.e. the sun, moon and stars, and all the ministering creatures which make their revolution in all the chariots of the heaven. In like manner twelve doors Uriel showed to me, open in the circumference of the sun's chariot in the heaven, through which the rays of the sun break forth: and from them is warmth diffused over the earth, when they are opened at their appointed seasons. As for the twelve portals in the heaven, at the ends of the earth, out of which go forth the sun, moon, and stars, and all the works of heaven in the east and in the west, there are many windows open to the left and to the right of them, and one window at its (appointed) season produces warmth, corresponding (as these do) to those doors from which the stars come forth according as He has commanded them, and wherein they set corresponding to their number. And I saw chariots in the heaven, running in the world, above those portals in which revolve the stars that never set. And one is larger than all the rest, and it is that that makes its course through the entire world.

And at the ends of the earth I saw twelve portals open to all the quarters ⟨of the heaven⟩, from which the winds go forth and blow over the earth. Three of them are open on the face (i.e. the east) of the heavens, and three in the west, and three on the right (i.e. the south) of the heaven, and three on the left (i.e. the north). And the three first are those of the east, and three are of the north, and three after those of the south, and three of the west. Through four of these come winds of blessing and prosperity, and from those eight come hurtful winds: when they are sent, they bring destruction on all the earth and on the water upon it, and on all who dwell thereon, and on everything which is in the water and on the land.

And the first wind from those portals, called the east wind, comes forth through the first portal which is in the east, inclining towards the south: from it comes forth desolation, drought, heat and destruction. And through the second portal in the middle comes what is fitting, and from it there come rain and fruitfulness and prosperity and dew; and through the third portal which lies toward the north come cold and drought.

And after these come forth the south winds through three portals; through the first portal of them inclining to the east comes forth a hot wind. And from the middle portal next to it there come forth fragrant smells, and dew and rain, and prosperity and health. And through the third portal lying to the west come forth dew and rain, and locusts and desolation.

And after these the north winds: from the seventh portal in the east come dew and rain, locusts and desolation. And from the middle portal come in a direct direction health and rain and dew and prosperity; and through the third portal in the west come cloud and hoar-frost, and snow and rain, and dew and locusts.

And after these are the west winds: through the first portal adjoining the north come forth dew and hoar-frost, and cold and snow and frost. And from the middle portal come forth dew and rain, and prosperity and blessing; and through the last portal which adjoins the south come forth drought and desolation, and burning and destruction. And the twelve portals of the four quarters of the heaven are therewith completed, and all their laws and all their plagues and all their benefactions have I shown to thee, my son Methuselah.

And the first quarter is called the east, because it is the first: and the second, the south, because the Most High will descend there, yea, there in quite a special sense will He who is blessed for ever descend. And the west quarter is named the diminished, because there all the luminaries of the heaven wane and go down. And the fourth quarter, named the north, is divided into three parts: the first of them is for the dwelling of men: and the second contains seas of water, and the abysses and forests and rivers, and darkness and clouds; and the third part contains the garden of righteousness.

I saw seven high mountains, higher than all the mountains which are on the earth: and thence comes forth hoar-frost, and days, seasons and years pass away. I saw seven rivers on the earth larger than all the rivers: one of them coming from the west pours its waters into the Great Sea. And these two come from the north to the sea and pour their waters into the Erythraean Sea in the east. And the remaining four come forth on the side of the north to their own sea, ⟨two of them to⟩ the Erythraean Sea, and two into the Great Sea and discharge themselves there. Seven great islands I saw in the sea and in the mainland: two in the mainland and five in the Great Sea.

And the names of the sun are the following: the first Orjârês, and the second Tômâs. And the moon has four names: the first is Asônjâ, the second Eblâ, the third Benâsê, and the fourth Erâe. These are the two great luminaries: their circumference is like the circumference of the heaven, and the size of the circumference of both is alike. In the circumference of the sun there are seven portions of light which are added to it more than to the moon, and in definite measures it is transferred till the seventh portion of the sun is exhausted. And they set and enter the portals of the west, and make their revolution by the north, and come forth through the eastern portals on the face of the heaven. And when the moon rises one fourteenth part appears in the heaven: on the fourteenth day she accomplishes her light. And fifteen parts of light are transferred to her till the fifteenth day ⟨when⟩ her light is accomplished, according to the sign of the year, and she becomes fifteen parts, and the moon grows by ⟨the addition of⟩ fourteenth parts. And in her waning ⟨the moon⟩ decreases on the first day to fourteen parts of her light, on the second to thirteen parts of light, on the third to twelve, on the fourth to eleven, on the fifth to ten, on the sixth to nine, on the seventh to eight, on the eighth to seven, on the ninth to six, on the tenth to five, on the eleventh to four, on the twelfth to three, on the thirteenth to two, on the fourteenth to the half of a seventh, and all her remaining light disappears wholly on the fifteenth. And in certain months the month has twenty-nine days, and once twenty-eight. And Uriel showed me another law: when light is transferred to the moon, and on which side it is transferred to her by the sun. During all the period during which the moon is growing in her light, she is transferring it to herself when opposite to the sun during fourteen days, and when she is illumined throughout, her light is accomplished full in the heaven. And on the first day she is called the new moon, for on that day the light rises upon her. She becomes full moon exactly on the day when the sun sets in the west, and from the east she rises at night, and the moon shines the whole night through till the sun rises over against her and the moon is seen over against the sun. On the side whence the light of the moon comes forth, there again she wanes till all the light vanishes and all the days of the month are at an end, and her circumference is empty, void of light. And three months she makes of thirty days, and at her time she makes three months of twenty-nine days each, in which she accomplishes her waning in the first period of time, and in the first portal for one hundred and seventy-seven days. And in the time of her going out she appears for three months ⟨of⟩ thirty days each, and for three months she appears ⟨of⟩ twenty-nine each. At night she appears like a man for twenty days each time, and by day she appears like the heaven, and there is nothing else in her save her light.

And now, my son, I have shown thee everything, and the law of all the stars of the heaven is completed. And he showed me all the laws of these for every day, and for every season of bearing rule, and for every year, and for its going forth, and for the order prescribed to it every month and every week: and the waning of the moon which takes place in the sixth portal: for in this sixth portal her light is accomplished, and after that there is the beginning of the waning: ⟨and the waning⟩ which takes place in the first portal in its season, till one hundred and seventy-seven days are accomplished: reckoned according to weeks, twenty-five and two days. She falls behind the sun and the order of the stars exactly five days in the course of one period, and when this place which thou seest has been traversed. Such is the picture and sketch of every luminary which Uriel the archangel, who is their leader, showed unto me.

And in those days the angel Uriel answered and said unto me: "Behold, I have shown thee everything, Enoch, and I have revealed everything to thee that thou shouldst see this sun and this moon, and the leaders of the stars of the heaven and all those who turn them, their tasks and times and departures."[5]

In spite of the poetic beauty of some passages, and the interesting evidence they afford of the scientific outlook of their period, there is a very clear difference between their

[5] Both this and the previous passage are translated by R. H. Charles, in Charles, vol. II, pp. 225, 237 following.

spirit and that of the Scriptures. To begin with, the mass of details ties the text closely to a particular philosophy of nature belonging to a given civilization, while the bare severity of Genesis is tied to no human "science". Again, in the texts we have quoted, God entrusts the care of his creation to a multitude of supernatural intermediaries, and not to man, as in the Bible. And lastly, the "great luminaries" are almost animated by an intelligence of their own: we are close to astrology. The part played by the human person, so strongly stressed in the Scriptures, is here very much reduced.

CHAPTER II

STORIES AND LEGENDS OF THE AGE OF THE PATRIARCHS

But it was not only educated men who felt the need to know more about the origins of the world and of man, and about their first ancestors. In the same way as we find among the products of other ancient civilizations, alongside cosmogonies of a philosophical kind, a sort of golden legend of the first ages of man, so we find in the apocrypha a large number of quasi-mythological stories concerning the first man and the first ages of mankind. Some merely expand the story told in Genesis. But there are others, either because of contamination from neighbouring civilizations, or because of Christian interpolations intended to strengthen and clarify the messianism of the Scriptures, which go well beyond what is in the Bible and include elements with an entirely different feeling and background.

I am not going to give even a rapid summary of this "para-history" in the apocrypha: a more precise notion of it will be given, I feel, by the quotation of a few of the more significant and typical texts.

Our writers were much concerned with Adam and Eve's transition from the supernatural life of the garden of Eden to their natural life on an earth now become hostile. We must remember that on this question not only Israel but the whole of antiquity took a general view exactly the opposite of our own: the passage to the state of man, *homo sapiens*, was not regarded as the crowning achievement of progressive evolution, but as a fall.

Such a view of things posed a number of problems: a prince in exile obliged to earn his living finds life more difficult than a victorious general raised to the throne.

From the various vicissitudes, suffered by our first parents in the change, I shall quote three, in passages from the *Book of the Penitence of Adam*: how they learned to dress themselves and to feed themselves, and how marriage was instituted (and in this last we may see the influence of Mazdaean dualism).

Bread

The word of the Lord came and said unto Adam: "Go down into the west of the cave until there you shall find a soil that is black and muddy, and there shall you find your food." And Adam heard the word of the Lord, and took Eve, and went down towards the black earth, and there found wheat in the ear, and the ears were ripe and good to eat. And Adam rejoiced in them. And the word of God came once again and said: "Take this wheat and make of it bread to strengthen your body." And God gave Adam the wisdom in his heart to prepare this wheat and make of it bread.

Clothing

And Adam and Eve took skins and came back to their treasure cave. And when they were returned there, they stood up and prayed, as was their wont. And long they thought how they should make themselves clothing from the skins, for they had no knowledge of this skill. Then God sent to them his angel to teach them all that they should do; and the angel said to Adam: "Go and bring the spines from the thorn-bush." And Adam did as the angel had bidden him. And the angel stretched the skins before him, and stuck the thorns into them, and prayed to God that they would remain fixed as he had put them. And so it happened by the command of God, and they dressed themselves in their clothes.

Marriage

Satan was filled with envy against them, and he and ten of his company took the form of maidens of incomparable beauty, and coming out of the waters of the river they came before Adam and Eve. And they said: "We desire to look upon the faces of Adam and Eve who are on the earth, and to see whether they are beautiful and whether they are different from our own." And they came upon the bank near to Adam and Eve; they saluted them and stood before them amazed, and Adam and Eve looked upon them and were astonished by their beauty, and said to them: "Is there then another world where there exist such beautiful creatures?" And the maidens answered and said to Adam and Eve: "There is, and we are but a part of a great number." And Adam said to them: "And what is it that has caused you thus to multiply?" And they answered: "We have men who marry us and we conceive and bear children, and our children grow and so our race is multiplied. And if you do not believe us, we can bring it about that you shall see our husbands and our children." And they called their husbands and their children, and men and children came up out of the water, and began each to go to his wife and to take his own children. And when Adam and Eve saw these things they were filled with amazement. And the maidens said to Adam and Eve: "You have seen our husbands and our children; and now Adam, you must do as we shall tell you so that you also shall have children and shall perpetuate your race." For Satan thought in his heart: "God forbade Adam to eat of the tree and Adam disobeyed his command and has suffered great punishment; and now I shall bring him to go in unto Eve without the command of God, and God will be wrath with him and will destroy him." But Adam thought he should offend God, and he fell to praying, as did Eve also, and Satan and his company plunged again into the waters, and

Adam and Eve returned to their cave as was their wont, and the hour of evening was come. And in the night they rose to pray, and Adam said: "Lord, thou knowest that we disobeyed thee, and through our fault our bodies have become as those of the brutes. Show us what is thy will, O Lord, and let not Satan come to trouble us with deceiving visions, lest we are led again to do that which will offend thee, so that thou art wrath with us and destroy us utterly." And God heard the words of Adam, and saw that they were true and that he was not able to resist the attacks of Satan; and the word of God came to Adam and said: "The pains thou now sufferest would never have come upon thee hadst thou not provoked my wrath, so that I drave thee from the garden."

And to Adam he sent the angel who had brought to him gold, and the angel who had brought to him incense, and him who had brought to him myrrh; and the angels said to Adam: "Take the gold and give it to Eve as a marriage gift, and make a covenant with her, and give her the incense as a pledge that thou and she shall be one flesh." And Adam heard the voice of the angel and took the gold and put it in the skirt of Eve's garment, and they made a covenant together, joining their hands. And the angels commanded Adam and Eve to pass forty days and forty nights in prayer, and then Adam might go in unto his wife, for then it would be in purity and not in impurity; and she should bear him children and they would fill and people the earth. And Adam and Eve heard the voice of the two angels, and the angels left them. And Adam and Eve fasted and prayed until the forty days were accomplished, and then they lay together as the angels had told them. And from the expulsion of Adam to the day when he wed Eve there were 223 days, that is, seven months and three days.

This filling and peopling of the earth, and the Flood, are both fully treated of, but it is generally only a matter of a detailed and wearisome amplification of the Bible story.

After the Flood, we enter proto-history: the world is very much as we know it: here are the birth of tribes and peoples and kingdoms, and the mysterious problem of the abandonment of the true God by men.

Let us see how the apocryphal writers explain the origin of idolatry. We know how suspicious Israel was of the idea of kingship,[1] and consequently we are struck by the assimilation of monarchy to idolatry in the following passage, also from the *Book of the Penitence of Adam*: the one is the direct cause of the other.

The Origins of Idolatry

(The children of Sem have become very numerous and have separated, divided into seventy-two tribes.)

And Raguel the firstborn son of Phaleg lived for two hundred and forty-two years, and died. And after one hundred and forty years of the life of Raguel, there was a man who ruled as king, and he was the first king on the earth, and he was called Nimrod the giant. This Nimrod saw under the heaven a fiery cloud, which was the work of Satan, and his heart was moved towards it, and he was amazed at its beauty, and called a craftsman called Santal and said to him: "Make me a crown of gold in the shape of that cloud." And he made such a crown, and Nimrod took it and set it upon his own head, and thereafter men said that a cloud had descended upon the head of Nimrod from the heaven. And he grew more and more wicked and mad until he thought in his heart that he was himself God. And Nimrod died in his two hundred and thirtieth year. And after him lived his son Saruch, in whose time and after the worship of stone idols spread through the world, and the children of men began to make stone idols, the first among them being Khaliton and Helidon. And the more the children of men multiplied over the earth, the more grew their wicked-

[1] Cf. 1 Kings 8. 4–8: "So all the elders of Israel met Samuel at Ramatha; Thou hast grown old, they said to him, and thy sons do not follow in thy footsteps. Give us a king, such as other nations have, to sit in judgement over us. It was little to Samuel's mind, this demand for a king to be their judge; but when he betook himself to the Lord in prayer, the Lord said to him, Grant the people all they ask of thee. It is my rule over them they are casting off, not thine."

ness, for they had neither law nor rule nor master whose teachings to follow. And they were crushed against the earth by him who ruled them, and strayed far from the ways of God. Each of them did as it pleased him, and they made idols of all kinds and prayed to them, and had no hope for the resurrection of the dead. When one of them died, they set upon his tomb an idol and said: "Here is his god; may he be propitious to him in his tomb." And they were accustomed to say of a dead man: "If the god on his tomb is powerful, his memory will not perish from the face of the earth." Satan it was who introduced this manner of speaking, and that is why the earth was full of idols, and those idols were of diverse shapes, male and female.

... And in that time, there dwelt in the city a rich man, who died. And his son made a golden image, in the likeness of his father, and set it upon his tomb, and commanded one of his slaves to stand by the idol, and sweep the ground about it, and sprinkle it with water, and burn incense. And when Satan saw this, he entered into the idol and spoke to the slave as if in the voice of the dead man. And a thief robbed the house of the rich man's son, and the son came to his father's tomb weeping and saying, "Father, a thief has stolen from me all that I possessed." And Satan answered from within the idol and said: "Be not distressed, but go and bring me here your son, and offer him to me a sacrifice, and I shall restore to you all that has been stolen." And the young man did to his son all that Satan had commanded. And straightway Satan entered into him and taught him magic and spells and soothsaying, and this was the first time that men took their children and offered them as a sacrifice to idols and to Satan.

Among all peoples, proto-history is the age of the heroes: Achilles and Aeneas, for example, who were no doubt real men, but were nearly gods, following their own extraordinary fates. We can be reasonably sure of their historical existence, and know that they played a determining part in the history of their peoples. But beyond that nothing is certain. Israel also had her great ancestors: they were the patriarchs, Abraham and his descendants. A whole book, *The Apocalypse of*

Abraham, was taken up with the story of the conversion of the father of all true believers. The twelve sons of Jacob, the founder of the twelve tribes, were believed to have left their last requests and commands in the *Testaments of the XII Patriarchs*.

Besides these, some of the mysterious personages who are mentioned in the Bible are described in the apocrypha with greater detail and in clearer relief. Let us take as an example the enigmatic Melchisedech: let us recall the verses of Genesis (14. 17–20):

> Thus he defeated Chodorlahomor, and the kings who were with him. And as he came back, the king of Sodom went out to meet him at the Valley of Savé, which is the same as the Royal Valley; Melchisedech, too, was there, the king of Salem. And he, priest as he was of the most high God, brought out bread and wine with him, and gave him this benediction, On Abram be the blessing of the most high God, maker of heaven and earth, and blessed be that most high God, whose protection has brought thy enemies into thy power. To him, Abram gave tithes of all that he had won.

What sort of man was this king to whom Abraham gave the tithes ordinarily reserved to the priests? How could there be a "priest of the most high God" outside the covenant made exclusively with Abraham and his seed? Israel was haunted by this unsolved problem. The Psalmist (109. 4) saw in Melchisedech a prefiguration of the priesthood of the Messias. More important still is what is said by the writer of the Epistle to the Hebrews. We know that the epistle is the work of a convert from Judaism in Alexandria in the first century A.D. He was therefore a brother in spirit and in his culture to the contemporary authors of most of the Old Testament apocrypha. There is the same nostalgia for Jerusalem and for the splendours of the Temple, the same uneasiness when faced with the apparent dissolution of the covenant. In this epistle, concerned with Christ the Son of God, the eternal priest, a long passage (7. 1–20) describes the eternal priesthood of Melchisedech, who had "no name of father or mother, no pedigree, no date of birth or of death; there he stands, eternally, a priest, the true figure of the Son of God."

The writers of the apocrypha took a different view. Melchisedech is given a genealogy and is linked with the great forefathers of Israel; but he is still the chosen of the most high God, the priest chosen by the Lord. We quote again from the *Book of the Penitence of Adam*:

> (Noe is dead.) . . . And after they had wept, the angel of the Lord appeared to Cainan: "Dost thou know me?" And he answered: "No, Lord." And the angel said to him: "I am the angel of the Lord; and he has sent me to you to bring you his command. Do not disobey the command of the Lord." And when Cainan heard these words of the angel he was amazed and said: "Speak, Lord." And the angel of the Lord spake thus: "I am he who brought to your father Adam the gold God granted to him in answer to his prayers when he spilt his blood upon the altar; I am the Angel Michael who received the soul of the just Abel; I am the angel who was with Sem, when he was born in the cave. . . . And since Noe has gone to his rest, I stay near to Sem, his first-born. And behold, God has sent me to you that I should take thy son Melchisedech and should lead him into the land where shall rest the body of your father Adam. And he shall be brought up in the sight of God; be not afflicted because of his going." And when Cainan heard these words of the angel, he fell on his face before him and said: "The Lord's will be done; I and my son are in thy hands, that he may do what he wills."
>
> And the angel of the Lord came that night to Melchisedech, who was sleeping, and appeared to him in the shape of a young man who tapped him on his right side and woke him from his sleep. And Melchisedech awoke and leapt up and saw that the chamber was filled with light and that a man was standing before him; and he was afraid, for he had never seen an angel. But the angel told him not to fear, girded his head and his breast and said to him: "Be not afraid; I am the angel of the

Lord, and he has sent me to you to bring you his commands, that you might accomplish the will of God." And Melchisedech said: "What is the command which you are charged with delivering to me?" And the angel said to him: "That you should go with the body of your father Adam to the middle of the earth and there, serving and honouring God, you should live in his sight, for God has chosen you from a child, since you are of the race of the blessed." And Melchisedech said: "Who will show me the body of my father Adam and who will carry it?" And the angel answered him: "Sem, the son of Noe, the grandfather of thy father." And the angel strengthened his heart, speaking to him for the space of an hour, inspiring him with courage and consoling him. And he said to him: "Reveal this mystery to no man unless it be to Sem, for fear lest the word spread and they take hold of the body of Adam and do not allow him to carry it to the land where God commanded it to lie." And the angel left him.

And the angel came to Sem, and said: "Arise and take the body of Adam as your father Noe commanded, and take Melchisedech with you, and go with him to the place where God commanded to you, and tarry not."

And when morning was come, Sem made a fine coffin and hid it near the Ark of the Covenant, and taking bread and wine and what he needed for a journey he came to Cainan and asked him for his son Melchisedech. Cainan began to tell him all that the angel had said to him, and joyfully gave him his son Melchisedech. And Sem said to Cainan: "Keep secret this mystery and reveal it to no-one." And Sem took Melchisedech, and they took a loaded ass and went to fetch the coffin. But they had no key with them to open the Ark, and they wondered how they should set about opening it. Then Sem came before the door and said to Melchisedech: "Open it, you who are great before God." Melchisedech obeyed him, and came near and touched the lock, and the door was immediately opened. And a loud voice came from the coffin crying: "Rejoice, O priest of the most high God, for you have been judged worthy to open the way for the priest of God, the first he made in this world." And this voice was of the Holy Spirit. And

Melchisedech was filled with emotion and said to Sem: "O Lord, I felt a breath of wind on my face and heard a voice, which spake unto me, but I saw nothing. That voice comes to us from the body of our father Adam." And Sem stood struck with amazement and knew not what he might answer. And while they stood thus struck with amazement, there came a voice from high in the heaven which said: "I am he who has chosen thee for my priest and who has brought thee here. Thou art worthy to carry the body of Adam, thou whom I have made priest, king and prophet." And Melchisedech went into the Ark and prayed and saluted the body of our father Adam, and carried it out, and the angel Michael helped him. And Sem also went into the Ark, and prayed, and took out the gold and incense and myrrh which he put with the body in the coffin which he had made, and closed it. And they closed the door of the Ark, as it had been before. And Sem took Melchisedech and the body of Adam, and set out on their journey, and the angel went with them. And he led them to the place where they should go. And they journeyed until evening, and came to a place where they desired to rest. And Melchisedech and Sem stood up to pray and while they were praying a voice came from the coffin wherein was the body of Adam and said: "Praise be to God who created me, who kept me in my life, who led me to death and is returning me to the earth from which he took me." And the voice blessed the young Melchisedech and said to him: "To no one of our race has God given the same grace as to you, and no priest has he consecrated with his hand except you, and I rejoice, my son, that the Lord has found you thus worthy." And Melchisedech was amazed to hear this voice which came from the body of Adam; for it happened because God willed it. And when Sem saw the marvels accomplished for Melchisedech, he was filled with such joy he could not contain it, and passed the whole night in praise of God, and prayed by the body of Adam until the morning. And when they came to difficult country, the angel carried them over it by the power of God and set them down on the other side, whether they were obstructed by mountains or by seas. And they journeyed thus until the end of the second day, and went down into a valley to rest. But Sem and Melchisedech felt no tiredness, for the strength of God was with them, but were joyful, as if they had just been to a wedding, and passed the whole night as before praying by the body of Adam. And there came a voice from the coffin which said to Melchisedech and to Sem: "Behold we have come to the place which was decreed by the Lord." And the voice said to Melchisedech: "In the country into which we are going the Word of God will come down and will suffer and will be crucified in the place where my body is laid, so that my skull will be watered with his blood. And in that hour my deliverance will be accomplished, and he will lead me into his kingdom and will give me my dignity of priest and pontiff." And the voice was silent, by the will of God, and Sem and Melchisedech were amazed at the voice which had spoken to them. And Melchisedech wept with joy, and remained in prayer until the day came. And they laid the body of our father Adam on an ass and continued on their way until they came to the decreed place. And then the angel stood before the ass and the coffin fell, but not as on the two first times with Melchisedech: it broke into two, and Sem and Melchisedech knew that this was the place designed by the will of God. And the angel left them to go back to the heaven, and said to God: "See, the body of Adam has come to the place you commanded; what would you have me do?" Then the word of the Lord came to the angel and said: "Go to Melchisedech and strengthen his heart, and command him to stay by the body of Adam, and when Sem is resting, command Melchisedech to go away and take with him all the bread and wine Sem has brought, and keep them."

The angel of the Lord came down, and taking the shape of a man appeared before Melchisedech and strengthened his heart, and said to Melchisedech: "Take the bread and the wine which Sem has brought." And he took them as the angel told him to. And they stayed by the body in prayer until the evening. And there came a great light above the body, and angels ascended and descended in the place where was the body of our father Adam. And they sang, full of gladness: "Blessings to thee, O Lord, who hast created the heaven and the earth and all the marvels that are therein." And the angels remained near the body of our father Adam until the morning came. And when the sun appeared, the voice of the Lord came to Melchisedech and spake unto him: "Rise, and take twelve stones, and make an altar, and set upon it the bread and the wine which Sem has brought, and make a communion between him and thee." And when Melchisedech heard the word of God, he hastened to do what God had commanded him. And when he set the offerings on the altar, he prayed to God that he might accept them. And the Holy Spirit descended on the sacrifice, and the mountain was filled with light. And then the angels said: "This offering has been accepted by the Lord; praise to him who has created men, and who has revealed great mysteries to them." And the Word of the Lord appeared to Melchisedech and said to him: "Behold I have made thee a priest; Sem and thou have made communion of the first sacrifice which thou hast offered. And as thou hast chosen twelve stones to build thine altar, so I shall choose twelve apostles to be the firm pillars of the world, and as thou hast built this altar, so I shall build myself an altar in the world."

If I have quoted this long extract in preference to others, it is because it seems typical of a certain aspect of the apocrypha, an aspect hardly developed in the centuries which are now our concern, but which developed almost to extravagance later: the desire for mystery, and for all that is mysterious, and the longing for teachings which were secret, alongside the official Scriptures. And it happened that the very terms of Genesis in the story of Melchisedech opened the door to this possibility.

The last part of the extract also shows how some early Christians filled out in their simple way a messianism which was not clear enough for their tastes in the inspired Scriptures.

Later, it was in the apocrypha which dealt with the origins of the world and with these very ancient times that the seeds of many heresies were found, but their errors are usually so gross that they are not worth dwelling long upon.

PART II

ISRAEL'S RESISTANCE

CHAPTER III

THE FORMS AND THE SPIRIT OF ISRAEL'S RESISTANCE

One of the most striking aspects of what the Bible does not tell us is its complete silence on the last centuries of the temporal history of Israel: for the story of the people of the Bible from the Return from Exile to the sack of Jerusalem by Titus we have to look for evidence outside the Scriptures.

Granted that we have now reached a fully historical period for which there is no lack of evidence, we shall not look in the apocrypha for a systematic account of the five centuries about which the Bible is silent; in any case, we should not find such an account. What we shall get from the apocryphal writers is rather evidence of how Israel reacted spiritually, the way in which Israel resisted foreign influence and domination.

The first thing we have to notice is the difference between Israel and all the other peoples around her.

It might be said that in a general way the idea of a transcendent divinity was not wholly wanting to the mind of antiquity, but that divinity was conceived of as so far removed from man that it had no real influence on religion, that is, on the relations between the human and the supernatural orders. Men addressed themselves to secondary deities, to gods of the harvest or of war, of the sea or of the woods, all arranged in a hierarchy about a national god, such as Zeus among the Greeks or Jupiter among the Romans.

In such a state of beliefs, it can easily be seen that at a time of conquest, the victorious nation could without difficulty absorb the gods of the conquered people. The hierarchy would change somewhat, one of the national gods having shown himself to be superior to the other. The other gods would find their place in an expanded pantheon. From such new relationships the general religious background would be enriched and widened, and often the gods thus "colonized" might find a new and fervent band of adherents among the conquerors. I might mention as an example the way the cult of Mithras became fashionable in the Roman armies, or the spread of the worship of Isis in certain circles in Greco-Roman society.

Israel was bound to be irreducibly opposed to such a pattern of behaviour. They had progressed beyond the notion of a national God long before the return from Exile: Yahweh was the one, transcendent God, the God of Abraham, Isaac and Jacob, it is true, but also the God of nations.

Again, man dealt directly with God himself. The pious Jew, just man or sinner, addressed his prayer directly to the Lord, with no intermediary divinity, no supernatural mediator. To God alone were sacrifices offered by the priests. It might be relevant to recall here how meagre is the angelology of the Bible: are angels personal beings, or is "angel" a name given to a manifestation of the Lord? It is difficult to give an answer to this question.[1] The apocrypha, on the other hand, mention angels constantly, and treat them as personal creatures charged with establishing and looking after the relations of man with the divinity.

We can understand, then, the astonishment of well-intentioned conquerors who prepared to sacrifice with great

[1] Cf. in this series: *What is an Angel?* by P.-R. Régamey, O.P.

pomp in the Temple in Jerusalem, only to be met with a violent and scandalized refusal.

This religious attitude had one practical consequence of great importance: Israel's idea of political power. In the Near East and in the Roman Empire the ideas of divine power and of human power were so interwoven that men had come to consider the ruler as an emanation from, or even an incarnation of, the divinity. For Israel political power came from God, it was delegated by God at his choice, and was clearly revocable; it changed nothing in the nature of the man possessing it, and there were plenty of examples of rulers chosen by God from whom, because of their injustice, God had turned his face, so that they then returned to their usual state, as weak and fallen sinners.

We could therefore say that as compared with the nations around her, and as compared with her conquerors, Israel had a secular conception of the civil power. Serious difficulties were bound to arise from this at the time of the Roman conquest. The emperor was the incarnation of the national divinity, and granted the importance of the Roman Empire tended to consider himself as *the* god of the world. To recognize his political power, and even to serve him zealously and submissively was more than merely insufficient: it was a sacrilege, it was a shocking manifestation of atheism (remember that the first Fathers of the Church, in the same spirit, had to defend the Christians against this same charge of atheism, precisely because they refused to worship the emperor).

So Israel, because she was what she was, was bound to be opposed to her conquerors. But with a few rare exceptions the Jewish people shrank from armed resistance. This nation, which had been so bellicose in its earlier days, continually at war attacking or defending itself against its neighbours, had sobered down considerably. On the one hand it must be admitted that Israel was not big enough any longer to fight against the great empires which rose and crumbled so rapidly;

and on the other hand, the descendants of the lions of old—think of the line of Judas Machabaeus—had not remained faithful to the spirit of their ancestors. In these conditions, the idea that it was for Yahweh himself to defend his people had prevailed over the naturally warlike propensities of earlier centuries.

But if the Lord was bound by the Covenant, Israel was no less so bound. If God seemed to have abandoned the seed of Abraham, could this not be because the people chosen first among the nations had been disloyal to the agreement made between God and the Father of the nation? Was it not wrong to think that the contest was between the armies of Cyrus or the Hellenistic kings and those of the Jews? God had abandoned Israel because Israel had abandoned God. It was not just a matter of a conflict of men: Jerusalem, unfaithful and adulterous, must do penance to be once again guarded and protected as a loyal spouse. The most sure defence of Israel was a return to the Covenant, the observation of the Law. We have seen this in its necessary result, the opposition and resistance of Israel to her invaders.

This outlook is expressed in an imaginative and moving way in the long text I am now going to quote. Written by an Alexandrian Jew of the first century A.D., it does not really correspond to its title, the *Third Book of Machabees*. The action takes place in Egypt in the third century B.C., when Ptolemy Philopator had just conquered his enemy Antiochus.[2]

> And when the Jews had sent to him some of the senate and elders to greet him, and bring him gifts, and congratulate him on what had happened, he became the more eager to visit them as quickly as possible. And when he had come to Jerusalem he sacrificed to the Most High God and offered thankofferings, acting in some measure according to what was suitable to the place. And entering into the holy place, and being struck by the care displayed, and the beauty, and admiring also the good

[2] Trans. C. W. Emmett, in Charles, vol. 1, pp. 163 ff.

order of the temple, it came into his mind to purpose to enter into the sanctuary. And when they said that this was not allowed, since not even members of their own nation could enter, or all the priests, but only the high priest who was chief of all, and he once a year, he was by no means convinced. And when the law had been read out to him, not even then did he desist from his claim that he himself should enter, saying, Even if they are deprived of this honour, I must not be so. And he asked why, when he entered into every shrine, none of those present hindered him? And some one answered thoughtlessly, that he did wrong to make this boast. But since this is so, he said, why should I not enter in any case, whether they wish it or not? Then the priests in all their robes fell down, and besought the Most High God to aid them in that which had come upon them, and to turn the violence of him who was making this wicked attack, filling the temple with lamentation and tears; and those who were left in the city hurried forth in confusion, concluding that something strange was happening. The virgins who had been shut up in their chambers rushed forth with their mothers, and covering their hair with dust and ashes, filled the streets with groanings and lamentations. And those who had been lately married, leaving the chambers prepared for wedded intercourse and forgetting their proper modesty, ran about in confusion through the city. And as for the new-born children, the mothers and nurses who had charge of them left them here and there, in the houses or in the streets without care, and came in crowds to the temple which is high above all. And manifold were the supplications of those gathered here because of the impious enterprise of the king. And with them the bolder from among the citizens would not endure his carrying the matter to an extremity, or his determination to complete his project; but calling on one another to rush to arms, and to die bravely for the law of their fathers, they made great confusion in the place, and being with difficulty turned from their purpose by the elders and the priests, they joined in supplication with them. And the multitude continued meanwhile praying as before. But the elders who were with the king tried in many ways to turn his haughty mind from the purpose he had conceived. But being emboldened and now setting them all aside, he was even beginning to approach, thinking that he would complete the design aforesaid. Therefore those that were with him seeing this, joined with our own people in beseeching him who has all power to defend them in their present need, and not to disregard the lawless and insolent deed. So incessant and vehement was the united cry of the multitude that an indescribable uproar arose. For it might have been thought that not only the people, but even the walls and the whole pavement were crying out, since all preferred death to the profanation of the holy place.

Then the High-Priest Simon bowing his knees before the holy place, and spreading out his hands in calm reverence, prayed after this manner: Lord, Lord, king of the heavens, and sovereign of all creation, holy among the holy ones, only ruler, almighty, give ear to us who are grievously troubled by one wicked and profane, made wanton in insolence and might. For thou who hast created all things, and governest the whole world, art a righteous ruler, and judgest those who do aught in violence and arrogance. Thou didst destroy those who aforetime did iniquity, among whom were giants trusting in their strength and boldness, bringing upon them a boundless flood of water. Thou didst burn up with fire and brimstone the men of Sodom, workers of arrogance, who had become known for all their crimes, and didst make them an example to those who should come after. Thou didst try with manifold and grievous punishments the insolent Pharaoh when he enslaved thy holy people Israel, and didst make known thy mighty power. And when he pursued with chariots and a multitude of peoples, thou didst overwhelm him in the depths of the sea, but those who trusted in thee, the ruler of all creation, thou didst bring safely through. And they seeing the works of thy hands, did praise thee, the almighty. Thou, O King, when thou didst create the boundless and measureless earth, didst choose this city and sanctify this place for thyself, who hast need of nothing, and didst glorify it by a splendid manifestation, establishing it to the glory of thy great and honourable name. And loving the house of Israel, thou didst promise that if there should be a falling away, and distress should overtake us, and we should come to this place and make our supplication, thou wouldst hear our prayer. And indeed thou art faithful and true. And seeing that oftentimes when our fathers were afflicted thou didst succour them in their humiliation, and didst deliver them from great evils, behold now, O holy king, for our many great sins we are grievously troubled and put into subjection to our foes, and faint in our weakness. In our low estate this insolent and profane man seeketh to do violence to the holy place which is consecrated upon earth to the name of thy glory. For man cannot reach thy dwelling-place, the heaven of heavens. But since thy good pleasure was in thy glory amongst thy people Israel, thou didst hallow this place. Punish us not by the uncleanness of these men, neither chastise us by their profane doings, lest the transgressors boast in their wrath or exult in the insolence of their tongue, saying, We have trodden down the house of the sanctuary as the houses of the abominations are trodden down. Blot out our sins and scatter abroad our offences and manifest thy mercy at this hour. Let thy compassion speedily overtake us, and put praises in the mouth of the fallen and broken in heart, granting us peace.

Then the God who beholds us all, the Father of all holy among the holy ones, hearing the supplication spoken according to the law, scourged him who was greatly uplifted in violence and insolence, shaking him to and fro as a reed by the wind, so that lying upon the ground powerless and paralysed in body he could not so much as speak, being smitten by a righteous judgement. Whereupon his friends and bodyguard, seeing that the chastisement which had overtaken him was swift, and fearing lest he should even die, speedily drew him out, being overwhelmed by an exceeding great fear. But having after some time recovered himself, he by no means came to repentance though he had been thus punished, but departed with bitter threats.

So, arriving in Egypt, and going on further in his wickedness, through his boon companions and associates, who have already been mentioned, utter strangers to all justice, he was not content with his countless excesses, but even reached such a pitch of insolence that he raised evil reports in those parts, and many of his friends watching carefully the royal purpose, themselves also followed his will. He purposed publicly to inflict a disgrace upon the Jewish nation, and erected a pillar on the tower in the palace with the inscription, That none who did not sacrifice should be allowed to enter their temples; and that all Jews should be degraded to the rank of natives and the condition of serfs, and that those who spoke against it should be taken by force and put to death; and that those who were registered should even be branded on their bodies with an ivy-leaf, the emblem of Dionysus, and be reduced to their former limited status. But that he might not appear an enemy to all, he added: But if any of them prefer to join those who are initiated into the mysteries, they shall have equal rights with the citizens of Alexandria.

Some readily gave themselves up, expecting to gain great glory from their association with the king. But the greater part stood firm with a noble courage, and departed not from their religion; and paying money as a ransom for their lives, fearlessly attempted to save themselves from the registration. And they remained of good hope that they should find help, and abhorred those who parted from them, accounting them as enemies of their nation, and excluding them from social intercourse, and the rendering of any service.

The impious king perceiving this was so greatly enraged that he was not only wrath with those who dwelt in Alexandria, but was even more bitterly hostile to those that dwelt in the country, and ordered that they should all be speedily gathered together, and put an end to by the most cruel death. While this was being arranged a most malicious report was noised abroad against the Jewish nation on the part of men who agreed together to do them hurt, an occasion being afforded for representing that they hindered them from the observance of the laws. But the Jews continued to maintain their goodwill towards the king and their unswerving fidelity. Yet worshipping God, and living according to his law, they held themselves apart in the matter of food; and for this reason they were disliked by some; but adorning their conversation by the good practice of righteousness they were established in the good report of all. But of this good practice, which was the common talk of all men with regard to the nation, the foreigners took no account; but they talked continually of the difference they made with regard to worship and food, alleging that they were friendly neither to the king nor his army, but ill-disposed, and bitterly hostile to his interests; and thus they cast no small opprobrium upon them. But the Greeks in the city having been in no way injured by them, seeing the unexpected disturbance about them, and the unlooked-for concourse, were not able to help them—for they lived under a tyranny—but tried to comfort them and were indignant, expecting that this affair would take a change for the better; for so great a community could not be thus allowed to perish when it had committed no fault. And already some of their neighbours and friends and business associates, taking aside some of the Jews secretly, gave pledges of their protection and earnest endeavours for their assistance.

So the king, puffed up by his present prosperity, and regarding not the power of the Most High God, but supposing that he himself would always hold firmly to the same purpose, wrote this letter against them. King Ptolemy Philopator to his generals and soldiers in Egypt and every place greeting and prosperity. I myself and our affairs prosper. Our expedition into Asia, of which you yourselves are aware, having been brought to an expected conclusion by the help of the gods granted us deliberately, we thought, not by force of arms, but by kindness and much benevolence to foster the peoples of Coele-Syria and Phoenicia, bestowing benefits upon them with all readiness. And having granted large revenues to the temples in the cities, we came to Jerusalem as well, going up thither to show honour to the temple of the accursed people who never cease from their folly. Seemingly they welcomed our presence, but their welcome was insincere; for when we were eager to enter their shrine and to honour it with magnificent and beautiful offerings, carried away by their ancient pride they prevented us from going in, being left unhurt by our power on account of the benevolence we have to all. But they showed plainly their ill-will towards us, and standing alone amongst nations in their stiff-necked resistance to kings and their own benefactors, they refuse to take anything in a proper spirit. We accommodated ourselves to their folly, and returning victoriously to Egypt, and treating all nations with kindness, have acted as was right. And under these circumstances, making known to all our ready forgiveness of their fellow-countrymen, on account of their alliance, and the numerous matters which have been freely entrusted to them from of old, we have ventured to make a change, and have made up our mind to hold them worthy even of Alexandrian citizenship, and to give them a share in our religious rites from time to time. But they taking this in the opposite spirit and rejecting the good offer with their inborn ill-feeling, and continually inclining to evil, not only refuse the invaluable citizenship, but also show their contempt silently and by words for the few among them who behave properly towards us, in every case secretly expecting that through their infamous behaviour we should speedily alter our policy. Therefore having good proof for our persuasion that they are evilly disposed towards us in every way, and taking precautions lest when some sudden tumult is raised against us hereafter we should have these impious people behind our backs as traitors and barbarous foes, we give order that, as soon as this epistle reaches you, you shall at once send to us with harsh and violent treatment those who dwell among you with women and children, binding them fast in every way with iron chains, to meet a terrible and ignominious death, as befits traitors. For we believe that when they have been punished together, our estate shall be established for the future in the surest and best condition. And whoever shall harbour any Jew, old man or child or very suckling, shall with all his house be tortured to death with the most horrible torments. Information may be given to anyone; the informer to receive the estate of the guilty party, with two thousand drachmae from the royal treasury, and to be honoured with freedom. And every place where a Jew shall be detected at all in concealment shall be made a waste and burnt with fire, and shall become entirely useless to any mortal creature for all time. Thus ran the letter.

In every place where this decree reached, a feast at the public charges was made for the heathen with exultation and joy, the hatred which had long before become inveterate in their hearts being now freely displayed. But among the Jews there was unceasing grief and a lamentable crying with tears, the heart being all aflame with their groanings, as they bewailed the unlooked-for destruction which had been suddenly decreed against them. What district or city or what habitable place at all or what streets were not filled with lamentation for them? For in such manner with harshness and pitiless heart were they sent away with one accord by the generals in the cities, that at the sight of their unusual sufferings even some of their enemies, with common pity before their eyes, remembering the uncertain issue of life, wept at their hapless departure. For there was carried away a multitude of old men, covered with their wealth of grey hairs, forcing to a swift journey their feet bent and sluggish from old age under the violence of their rough driving which knew no shame. And the young women who had but lately entered the marriage chamber for the society of wedded life, with lamentations instead of joy, and with their perfumed locks covered with dust, were carried away unveiled, and with one accord sang a dirge in place of the wedding hymn, scarred by the cruel treatment of the heathen; and as prisoners exposed to public gaze they were dragged along with violence until they were embarked on board. And their consorts, with ropes on their necks instead of garlands, in the flower of their youthful age, spent the remainder of the days of their marriage feast in dirges instead of mirth and youthful ease, seeing the grave already yawning at their feet. And they were brought on board driven like wild beasts under the constraint of iron bonds; some were fastened by the neck to the benches of the ships; others had their feet secured by the strongest fetters; and further they were shut off from the light by the thick planks above, that in entire darkness they might be treated as traitors throughout the whole voyage.

When they had been brought to the place called Schedia, and the voyage was completed as determined by the king, he ordered them to be imprisoned in the hippodrome that was before the city, a place of immense circuit and very suitable for making them into a gazing stock to all who entered the city, and to those of the inhabitants who went into the country to sojourn, so that they might neither communicate with his army, nor in any way claim protection of the walls. But after this had been done, hearing that their fellow-countrymen in the city often went out in secret and bewailed the shameful fate of their brethren, he was enraged and ordered that they should be treated in exactly the same way as the others, receiving in no respect a lesser punishment. And he commanded that the whole race should be registered by name, not for the wearisome service of labour which was briefly described before, but that they should be tortured with the torments to which he had sentenced them, and finally be made an end of in the space of a single day. The registration therefore was carried on with bitter haste and zealous diligence from sunrise to sunset, coming to an end after forty days but still uncompleted.

But the king was greatly and continually filled with joy, ordering feasts in the temples of his idols, with a heart far astray from the truth and profane lips, praising dumb idols which could not speak to them or help, and uttering words which were not fitting against the most high God. But after the aforesaid space of time the scribes reported to the king that they were no longer able to continue the registration of the Jews on account of their incalculable number; although the greater number of them were still in the country, some still remaining in their homes and others on the journey, it was impossible for all the generals in Egypt. And after he had threatened them fiercely as having been bribed to contrive their escape, he was at length clearly convinced on this point, when they told him and proved that even the paper manufactory and the pens which they used for writing had already given out. But this was the working of the invincible providence of him who was aiding the Jews from heaven.

Then he called Hermon who was in charge of the elephants, and filled with bitter anger and wrath, and altogether inflexible, ordered him for the next day to drug all the elephants—in number five hundred—with copious handfuls of frankincense, and abundance of unmixed wine, and then when they were maddened by the plentiful supply of drink to bring them in to compass the fate of the Jews. And giving this order he turned to his feasting, having gathered together those of his friends and army who were most hostile to the Jews, while the ruler of the elephants attended to the injunction with all care. And the servants who were in charge of the Jews went out in the evening and bound the hands of the hapless wretches, taking all other precautions to keep them safe through the night, imagining that the nation would at one blow meet its final destruction. But the Jews who seemed to the heathen to be destitute of all protection, on account of the constraint and bonds which encompassed them on every side, with crying that would not be silenced, all called with tears on the almighty Lord and ruler of all power, their merciful God and father, beseeching him to frustrate the wicked design against them and to deliver them by a glorious manifestation from the fate yawning ready before them. So their prayer ascended fervently to heaven; but Hermon, having given the pitiless elephants drink till they were filled with the plenteous supply of wine and sated with frankincense, came early in the morning to report to the king about this. But the good creature, bestowed night and day from the beginning of time by him who gives the portion of sleep to all, even to whomsoever he will, this he sent upon the king; and he was overborne by a sweet and heavy slumber by the operation of the Lord, thus being greatly foiled in his lawless purpose, and utterly disappointed in his unchangeable design. But the Jews having escaped the appointed hour praised their holy God, and again besought him who is ready to forgive to manifest the might of his all-powerful hand before the proud eyes of the heathen. But when the middle of the tenth hour had nearly come he who was in charge of the invitations, seeing the guests assembled, went to the king and shook him. And having woken him up with difficulty, he pointed out that the hour of the banquet was already passing, reminding him of the circumstances. And the king considering these, betook himself to his cups and ordered those who had come to the banquet to take their places over against him. And when this had been done he called upon them to give themselves up to revelry, and counting themselves highly honoured to reckon as a joy the feast, late as it was. And when the entertainment had gone on for some time, the king called Hermon and asked with fierce threats why the Jews had been allowed to survive that day. But when he pointed out that he had completely carried out the order overnight, and his friends confirmed him, the king with a rage more fierce than Phalaris said that the Jews might thank his sleep for the respite of the day; but, he added, make ready the elephants in the same manner without further delay for the following day to destroy utterly the accursed Jews. When the king had spoken, all who were present readily assented with joy with one accord, and each one departed to his own house. But they did not spend the night season in sleep, so much as in devising all manner of cruel insults for those whom they thought to be in such a wretched plight.

So soon as the cock had crowed in the morning, Hermon harnessed the beasts and began to put them in motion in the great colonnade. And the multitudes in the city assembled for the piteous spectacle, eagerly looking for the break of day. But the Jews drawing their last breath for but a brief moment more, with tearful supplications and strains of woe, raising their hands to heaven, besought the Most High God again to help them speedily. The rays of the sun were not yet scattered abroad, and the king was receiving his friends, when Hermon came to his side and invited him to go forth, explaining that the desire of the king was ready to be fulfilled. When the king understood him, he was astonished at the unusual summons to go forth, having been overwhelmed with complete ignorance, and asked what was the matter on account of which this had been so zealously completed. But this was the operation of God the ruler of all, who had put in his mind forgetfulness of his former devices. But Hermon and all his friends pointed to the beasts and the army; It is prepared, O king, according to thine eager purpose. But he was filled with fierce anger at the words, because by the providence of God he had entirely lost his wits on this matter, and looking on him said threateningly, If thy parents or offspring were here, I would have furnished them as this rich banquet for the fierce beasts in place of the Jews against whom I have no charge and who have shown in a pre-eminent degree a full and unshaken loyalty to my ancestors. And indeed, if it were not for the affection kindled by our life together and thy service, thou shouldst have died instead of these. So Hermon met with an unexpected and dangerous threat, and his eyes and countenance fell. And the king's friends, slinking away sullenly one by one, sent away the assembled crowds, each to his own business. And the Jews hearing the words of the king, praised the Lord God who had manifested his glory, the king of kings, having obtained this help also from him.

But the king, having arranged the banquet once more in the same way, ordered them to turn to their pleasures. And calling Hermon he said threateningly, How often, thou wretched creature, must I give thee orders about these very things? Even now make ready the elephants for the morrow to destroy the Jews. But his kinsmen who sat at table with him wondered at his shifting purpose, and remonstrated, How long, O King, dost thou make trial of us as though we were fools, now for the third time giving orders for their destruction, and once more when the matter is in hand changing and cancelling thy decree? Wherefore the city is in a tumult through its expectation, and being crowded with throngs of people has now been several times in danger of being put to plunder. On this the king, a Phalaris in all things, was filled with madness, and, reckoning nothing of the changes of mind which had been wrought in him for the protection of the Jews, swore strongly a fruitless oath that he would without delay send to the grave the Jews mangled by the knees and feet of the beasts, and would march against Judaea and quickly level it to the ground with fire and sword, and burning to the earth their temple which he might not enter would quickly make it empty for all time of those who sacrificed therein. Then his friends and kinsmen went away joyfully with good confidence, and ordered the army to the most convenient places of the city to keep guard. And the ruler of the elephants, having driven the beasts into a state almost, one might say, of madness by fragrant draughts of wine mingled with frankincense, and having fitted them in a fearful guise with implements, at dawn, the city being now filled with countless multitudes thronging towards the hippodrome, entered the palace and urged on the king to the business that lay before him. And he, his impious heart filled with fierce anger, started forth with all his force with the beasts, determined with an unfeeling heart and his own eyes to gaze on the piteous and grievous destruction of the aforementioned Jews. And when they saw the dust raised by the elephants going out at the gate, and the armed force accompanying them, and the movement of the crowd, and heard the far-sounding tumult, thinking that the last crisis of their life had come and the end of their miserable suspense, they betook themselves to lamentation and groans, and kissed one another, embracing their relatives and falling on their necks, parents and children, mothers and daughters; and others with new-born babes at their breast drawing their last milk. But none the less, reflecting on their former deliverances sent from heaven, with one accord they threw themselves on their faces, and took the babies from their breasts, and cried out with an exceeding loud voice, beseeching the ruler of all power by a manifestation to show pity upon them now that they were come to the gates of death.

But a certain Eleazar, a man of note among the priests of the country, whose years had already reached old age, and who was adorned with every virtue of life, made the elders who were round him cease from calling on the holy God, and prayed thus: King of great power, most high, almighty God, who governest all creation with loving-kindness, look upon the seed of Abraham, the children of Jacob thy sanctified one, the people of thy sanctified inheritance, who are unjustly perishing, strangers in a strange land. O Father, thou didst destroy Pharaoh, the former ruler of this Egypt, with his multitude of chariots, when he was lifted high in his lawless insolence and a tongue speaking great things, drowning him and his proud host, and didst cause the light of thy mercy to shine upon the race of Israel. Thou, when Sennacherib, the cruel king of the Assyrians, was puffed up by his countless hosts, after he had taken the whole earth captive by his sword, and was lifted up against thy holy city speaking grievous words of boasting and insolence, thou, Lord, didst break him in pieces, making manifest thy power to many nations. Thou, when the three friends in Babylonia freely gave their life to the flames that they should not serve vain things, didst make as dew the fiery furnace, and deliver them unharmed even to the hair of their head, turning the flame upon all their adversaries. Thou, when Daniel was cast through the slanders of envy to the lions beneath the ground as food for wild beasts, didst bring him up to the light unhurt. And when Jonah was languishing unpitied in the belly of the sea-born monster, thou didst restore him, O Father, uninjured to all his household. And now thou hater of insolence, rich in mercy, protector of all, quickly manifest thyself to the saints of Israel's line, in their insolent oppression by the abominable and lawless heathen. And if our life has been ensnared by impious deeds during our sojourning, save us from the hand of the enemy, and destroy us, O Lord, by whatever fate thou choosest. Let not the men whose thoughts are vanity bless their vain gods for the destruction of thy beloved, saying, Neither has their God delivered them. Thou who hast all might and all power, the Eternal, look now upon us; pity us who by the mad insolence of lawless men are being sent to death as traitors; and let the heathen today fear thy invincible might, thou glorious one, who hast mighty works for the salvation of the race of Israel. The whole multitude of babes with their parents beseecheth thee with tears. Let it be shown to all heathen that thou art with us, O Lord, and hast not turned thy face away from us; but as thou hast said, Not even when they were in the land of their enemies have I forgotten them, even so bring it to pass, O Lord.

And when Eleazar was even now ending his prayer, the king with the beasts and the whole insolent array of his army came to the hippodrome. And the Jews beholding it raised a great cry to heaven, so that now the surrounding valleys re-echoed it, and caused in all the hosts an incontrollable trembling. Then the greatly glorious, almighty, and true God, making manifest his holy face, opened the gates of heaven, from which two glorious angels of terrible aspect descended, visible to all but the Jews, and withstood them and filled the army of the adversaries with confusion and terror, and bound them with immovable fetters. And a great horror seized on the body of the king as well, and his fierce insolence was forgotten. And the beasts turned round against the armed hosts that followed them and began to tread them underfoot and destroy them.

And the king's wrath was turned to pity and tears on account of that which he had devised before. For hearing the outcry and seeing them all prostrate to meet their death, he wept and angrily threatened his friends, saying, Ye usurp the kingly power, surpassing even tyrants in your cruelty; and me myself, who am your benefactor, ye plot to deprive of my dominion and my life, devising secretly things which are unprofitable to the kingdom. Who hath driven each one from his home the men who have faithfully held the fortresses of our country, and gathered them here without reason? Who hath thus lawlessly overwhelmed with indignities those who from the beginning have been in all things conspicuous beyond all nations in their goodwill towards us, and have ofttimes encountered the worst dangers man can undergo? Loose, yea loose, their unjust bonds; send them to their homes in peace, asking pardon for what has been already done. Set free the sons of the almighty living God of heaven, who from the days of our ancestors until now hath granted an unimpaired stability and glory to our estate. Thus he spake; and they, having been set free in a moment, praised the holy God their saviour, having but now escaped death.

Even if the story did not always really end so happily, this example still bears genuine witness to Israel's staunch resistance to her conquerors' totalitarian rule, despite her good intentions towards political authority. This small, uncrushable pocket of resistance inevitably and swiftly excited the conquerors' anger, and we shall now see, from the apocrypha, how the Jewish people tried in their daily lives effectively to defend the spirit of Israel.

CHAPTER IV

EXTERNAL AND INTERNAL RESISTANCE

We have seen the magnitude of the disaster that fell upon Israel from the third century B.C. on, and which could only increase as time passed. At the time of the Exile in Babylon—always the point of reference in bad times—the Jews had been carried off to a foreign land, but they had soon found in Cyrus an understanding protector: the punishment sent by the Most High thus lasted no longer than a long lifetime. But from the time of the Hellenistic conquests on, there was a crescendo of catastrophes which grew daily more terrible. At first, if the Jews did lose their national sovereignty, they none the less retained some degree of independence, and their fate was no different from that of other small states around them. Nationalism was far from dead, but gradually all minds were seized with the idea that only the Lord himself would re-establish his kingdom. What then struck pious Jews with horror was to see the inward degeneration of the chosen people, to see the descendants of Judas Machabaeus coming to terms with pagans, and the priestly caste (the Sadducees) converted to foreign customs and ideas; then the conquerors themselves became one after another more and more hostile to the Jewish religion itself: first the tolerant Lagoids, then the Seleucids and their policy of Hellenization, and lastly Rome, the Beast, with its compulsory worship of the Caesars and its ferocious and total reprisals.

As we read the apocrypha, we can distinguish the several principal attitudes adopted by the Jews in reaction to this unhappy situation. The first is that of grief and despair: "How could you abandon us, O Lord?" Second, there was a return to the terms of the Covenant, to the strictest observance of the Law. But there were some who went further than this, and put their trust in a conversion of the heart and an unconditional faith in the Most High:[1]

> So thou gavest thy city over into the hands of thine enemies. Then I said in my heart: Are their deeds any better that inhabit Babylon? Has he for this rejected Sion? It came to pass when I came hither and saw ungodly deeds innumerable, and myself saw many sinners these thirty years, that my heart was perturbed; for I have seen
>
> how thou dost suffer the sinners
> and dost spare the ungodly,
> how thou hast destroyed thy people
> and preserved thine enemies;
>
> and hast not made known at all unto any how this course of thine shall be abandoned. Have the deeds of Babylon been better than those of Sion? Has any other nation known thee beside Israel? Or what tribes have so believed thy covenants as those of Jacob? Whose reward nevertheless hath not appeared nor their labour borne fruit! For I have gone hither and thither through the nations and seen them in prosperity, although unmindful of thy commandments. Now therefore weigh thou our iniquities, and those of the inhabitants of the world, in the balance and so shall be found which way the turn of the scale inclines. Or when was it that the inhabitants of the earth did not sin before thee? Or what nation hath so kept thy precepts? Individual men of note indeed thou mayest find to have kept thy precepts; but nations thou shalt not find.

[1] 4 Ezra, trans. G. H. Box, in Charles, vol. II, pp. 563 ff.

Thereupon the angel answered me who had been sent to me, and whose name was Uriel; and he said to me: Thy heart hath utterly failed thee regarding this world; and thinkest thou to comprehend the way of the Most High?...

I meant not to ask about the ways above but of those things we daily experience;

Why is Israel to the heathen given over for reproach,
thy beloved people to godless tribes given up?
The Law of our fathers has been brought to destruction,
the written covenants exist no more;
We vanish from the world as locusts,
our life is as a breath.

We indeed are not worthy to obtain mercy; but what will he do for his own name whereby we are called?...

And out of all the peoples who have become so numerous thou hast gotten thee one people: and the law which thou didst approve out of all laws thou hast bestowed upon the people whom thou didst desire.

And now, O Lord, why hast thou delivered up the one unto the many, and dishonoured the one root above the rest, and scattered thine only one among the multitude?

And why have they who denied thy promises been allowed to tread underfoot those that have believed thy covenants? If thou didst so much hate thy people they ought to have been punished with thine own hands...

Of very grief I have spoken; for every hour I suffer agonies of soul in striving to comprehend the way of the Most High, and to seek out the decree of his judgement.

For there were still just men in Israel; and as Abraham prayed for Sodom and Gomorrha, could not they draw down from heaven the salvation of their people?

O look not on the sins of thy people,
but on them that have served thee in truth;
Regard not the deeds of the godless,
but rather them that have kept thy covenants in tortures;

Think not upon those that have walked in devious ways before thee,
but remember them that have willingly recognized thy fear;
Will not to destroy those that have lived like cattle,
but regard them that have gloriously taught thy Law;
Be not wrath with those that are deemed worse than the beasts,
but love them that have always put their trust in thy glory—
For we and our fathers have passed our lives in ways that bring death: but thou, because of us sinners, are called compassionate. For if thou hast a desire to compassionate us who have no works of righteousness, then shalt thou be called "the gracious One". For the righteous, who have many works laid up with thee, shall out of their own deeds receive their reward—
But what is man that thou shouldst be wrath with him?
Or what is a corruptible race that thou canst be so bitter towards it?
For in truth
There is none of the earth-born who has not dealt wickedly,
and among those that exist who has not sinned.
For in this, O Lord, shall thy righteousness and goodness be declared, if thou wilt compassionate them that have no wealth of good works.

But the Lord seemed deaf to the supplications of the just. Nevertheless, and this cry is heard often in the apocrypha, surely it was with Israel that God made his Covenant? The Lord must be true to his word, so it must have been Israel that broke the alliance, through sinners who broke the law, and went to the gymnasia naked like Greeks and took foreign wives. Their sins were clear for all to see, and nothing could be more natural than that the Lord should turn away from them, and that they should die terrible deaths, like Herod the Great. But were the righteous fervent enough and strict enough in their observance to outweigh such horrors as these?

So were born the "Pharisees", so frequently stigmatized in the Gospels. When the descendants of Judas Machabaeus were seen to lack the spirit of their forefather, those who had supported them, the Chasidim, deserted them and withdrew from the official affairs of the nation. They made a new sect, fervently nationalist and exaggeratedly ritualistic.

Nationalism and ritualism: the persecutions suffered by the Jews had encouraged the confusion of these two ideas. In their desire for complete assimilation, the conquerors had attacked the Jewish way of life, wholly governed as it was by the Law. Obedience to the Lord's commandments (and those added over the years by the scribes) was the mark of the righteous man, and it was also the mark of a man's refusal to submit to the ministers of the Beast—the invader—who forbade circumcision or the observance of the sabbath, but encouraged mixed marriages as an excellent means of colonization.

Now such a reaction was doubtless a kind of treason on the spiritual level, which is why Christ often attacked the Pharisees during his ministry. But on the human, and even on the religious level, it had some greatness of its own. It was born of the martyrs and great leaders who left their names in Israel's history, and it produced some of the finest passages in the apocrypha.

Indeed, it was altogether necessary that the Israelites, in the historical context just described, should feel proud of themselves, and of their history and traditions. If they did not, they became no more than a conquered people, cut off from the world by an obsolete particularism doomed to disappear. But the spirit of the Chasidim was quite other: and we have clear and definite evidence of that spirit in the *Book of Jubilees.* It is a history of the world, told to Moses, parallel to the account in Genesis and Exodus. The matter of the book would be of little interest, were it not presented in a very biassed, even tendentious, manner. The object was to prove that the Jewish ritual was of great antiquity, and was, so to speak, of the nature of man; to show that Israel was not, beside its brilliantly civilized neighbours, a sort of "under-developed country", but that her traditions were venerable and triumphed over time.

We might compare the author with the descendant of a noble and ancient family who sees his children tempted by the comfortable, even luxurious, villas of the Côte d'Azur, and tells them the story of his house, even going so far as to justify its discomforts by saying that they date back to the crusades. So our author, wanting to justify all the rabbinical commandments, and using over-historical arguments, allows us to see, even though the story he tells is one of God's guidance, the spiritual desiccation such an attitude necessarily produced.

I shall quote some passages relating to the most important precepts, beginning with the sabbath, prescribed for the angels themselves:[2]

> And He gave us a great sign, the Sabbath day, that we should work six days, but keep Sabbath on the seventh day from all work. And all the angels of the presence, and all the angels of sanctification, these two great classes—He hath bidden us to keep the Sabbath with Him in heaven and on earth. And He said unto us: "Behold, I will separate unto Myself a people from among all the peoples, and these shall keep the Sabbath day, and I will sanctify them unto Myself as My people, and will bless them; as I have sanctified the Sabbath day and do sanctify it unto Myself, even so will I bless them, and they shall be My people and I will be their God. And I have chosen the seed of Jacob from amongst all that I have seen, and have written him down as My first-born son, and have sanctified him unto Myself for ever and ever; and I will teach them the Sabbath day, that they may keep Sabbath thereon from all work." And thus He created therein a sign in accordance with which they should keep Sabbath with us on the seventh day, to eat and to drink, and to bless Him who has created all things as He has blessed and sanctified unto Himself a peculiar people

[2] Book of Jubilees, trans. R. H. Charles, in Charles, vol. II, pp. 14 ff.; p. 82.

above all peoples, and that they should keep Sabbath together with us. And He caused His commands to ascend as a sweet savour acceptable before Him all the days. . Wherefore do thou command the children of Israel to observe this day that they may keep it holy and not do thereon any work, and not to defile it, as it is holier than all other days. And whoever profanes it shall surely die, and whoever does thereon any work shall surely die eternally, that the children of Israel may observe this day throughout their generations, and not be rooted out of the land; for it is a holy day and a blessed day. And everyone who observes it and keeps Sabbath thereon from all his work, will be holy and blessed throughout all days like unto us... For that day is more holy and blessed than any jubilee day of the jubilees; on this we kept Sabbath in the heavens before it was made known to any flesh to keep Sabbath thereon on the earth. And the Creator of all things blessed it, but He did not sanctify all peoples and nations to keep Sabbath thereon, but Israel alone: them alone He permitted to eat and drink and to keep Sabbath thereon on the earth.

Ye shall do no work whatever on the Sabbath day save what ye have prepared for yourselves on the sixth day; so as to eat, and drink, and rest, and keep Sabbath from all work on that day, and to bless the Lord your God, who has given you a day of festival and a holy day: and a day of the holy kingdom for all Israel is this day among their days for ever. For great is the honour which the Lord has given to Israel that they should eat and drink and be satisfied on this festival day, and rest thereon from all labour which belongs to the labour of the children of men, save burning frankincense and bringing oblations and sacrifices before the Lord for days and for Sabbaths. This work alone shall be done on the Sabbath-days in the sanctuary of the Lord your God; that they may atone for Israel with sacrifice continually from day to day for a memorial well-pleasing before the Lord, and that He may receive them always from day to day according as thou hast been commanded. And every man who does any work thereon, or goes a journey, or tills his farm, whether in his house or any other place, and whoever lights a fire, or rides on any beast, or whoever catches an animal or a bird or a fish, or whoever fasts or makes war on the Sabbaths: The man who does any of these things on the Sabbath shall die, so that the children of Israel shall observe the Sabbaths according to the commandments regarding the Sabbaths of the land, as it is written in the tablets, which He gave into my hands that I should write out for thee the laws of the seasons, and the seasons according to the divisions of their days.

Circumcision, the sign of the chosen people:[3]

And everyone that is born, the flesh of whose foreskin is not circumcised on the eighth day, belongs not to the children of the covenant which the Lord made with Abraham, but to the children of destruction; nor is there, moreover, any sign on him that he is the Lord's, but he is destined to be destroyed and slain from the earth, and to be rooted out of the earth, for he has broken the covenant of the Lord our God. For all the angels of the presence and all the angels of sanctification have been so created from the day of their creation, and before the angels of the presence and the angels of sanctification He hath sanctified Israel and let them observe the sign of this covenant for their generations as an eternal ordinance, and they will not be rooted out of the land. For the command is ordained for a covenant, that they should observe it for ever among all the children of Israel. For Ishmael and his sons and his brothers and Esau, the Lord did not cause to approach Him, and He chose them not because they are the children of Abraham, because He knew them, but He chose Israel to be His people. And He sanctified it, and gathered it from amongst all the children of men; for there are many nations and many peoples, and all are His, and over all hath He placed spirits in authority to lead them astray from Him. But over Israel He did not appoint any angel or spirit, for He alone is their ruler, and He will preserve them and require them at the hand of His angels and His spirits, and at the hand of all His powers in order that He may preserve them and bless them, and that they may be His and He may be theirs from henceforth for ever.

[3] *Op. cit.*, pp. 36–37.

And there will no more be pardon or forgiveness unto them for all the sin of this eternal error.

As for mixed marriages, the author has to forbid them, and to base his prohibition on the patriarchal tradition; so he goes so far as to praise the murder of the men of Sichem by Simeon and Levi, even though Jacob, their father, reproached them with it on his deathbed (Gen. 48. 22).

We can see, then, that this first reaction, however brave and worthy it was, did not happen without a profound betrayal of the very spirit of the Bible. We can understand the attitude of Christ to the Pharisees. And we can also imagine how more spiritually holy minds—isolated minds—could not sympathize with this somewhat primitive reaction, but sought other ways of preserving their loyalty to the Covenant and the spirit of Israel. Not that their starting-point was so very different: they shared the same stupefaction at Israel's temporal annihilation, the same unconditional trust in the Lord, the same mistrust of purely human methods—war and violence. But while those simple minds who had followed Judas Machabaeus had only reacted by exaggerating and complicating their particularism, those Jewish minds who had gone further than this tried to learn from what was happening a more universal way of living and praying and thinking.

The first problem that arose was that of hope and trust in the divine protection, the other side of which was that of the apparent abandonment of his people by God. Belief in the covenant made with Abraham was ineradicably certain: whatever their provenance, the apocryphal books are at one in this appeal made to God for the guidance and protection he had always granted his people.[4]

And I said: O Lord my Lord, was it not thou who in the beginning, when thou didst form the earth—and that thyself alone—didst speak and commandedst the dust, so that it gave

[4] 4 Ezra, trans. G. H. Box, in Charles, vol. II, pp. 562 ff.

thee Adam, a lifeless body? But yet it was both itself the formation of thy hands and thou breathedst into him the breath of life, so that he was made living before thee. And thou leddest him into Paradise, which thy right hand did plant before ever the earth came forward; and to him thou commandedst only one observance of thine, but he transgressed it. Forthwith thou appointedst death for him and for his generations, and from him were born nations and tribes, peoples and clans innumerable. And every nation walked after their own will, and behaved wickedly before thee, and were ungodly—but thou didst not hinder them. Nevertheless again in due time thou broughtest the Flood upon the earth and upon the inhabitants of the world, and destroyedst them. And their fate was one and the same; as death overtook Adam, so the Flood overwhelmed these. Nevertheless one of them thou didst spare—Noah with his household and with him all the righteous his descendants. And it came to pass that when the inhabitants upon the earth began to multiply, and there were born children also and peoples and nations many, that they began to practise ungodliness more than former generations. And it came to pass that when they practised ungodliness before thee, thou didst choose thee one from among them whose name was Abraham: him thou didst love, and unto him only didst thou reveal the end of the times secretly by night; and with him thou didst make an everlasting covenant, and didst promise him that thou wouldst never forsake his seed. And thou gavest him Isaac, and to Isaac thou gavest Jacob and Esau. And thou didst set apart Jacob for thyself, but Esau thou didst hate; and Jacob became a great host. And it came to pass that when thou leddest forth his seed out of Egypt, and didst bring them to the Mount Sinai,

Thou didst bow down the heavens,
  didst make the earth quake
  and convulsedst the world—
Thou didst cause the deeps to tremble
  and didst alarm the spheres.
And thy glory went through the four gates of fire, earthquake, wind and cold,

To give Law to Jacob's seed
and commandment to the generation of Israel.

And yet thou didst not take away from them the evil heart, that thy Law might bring forth fruit in them . . . and then thou didst raise up for thyself a servant whose name was David; and thou commandedst him to build the City which is called after thy name, and to offer thee oblations therein of thine own. And after this had been done many years, the inhabitants of the City committed sin.

The Jews found again the voice of David to sing of their laments, and their hopes and—despite all appearances—the glory of the Lord:[5]

When the sinner waxed proud, with a battering-ram he cast down fortified walls,
And Thou didst not restrain him.
Alien nations ascended Thine altar,
They trampled it proudly with their sandals;
Because the sons of Jerusalem had defiled the holy things of the Lord,
Had profaned with iniquities the offerings of God.
Therefore He said: Cast them far from Me;

. . . .

It was set at naught before God,
It was utterly dishonoured;
The sons and the daughters were in grievous captivity,
Sealed was their neck, branded was it among the nations.
According to their sins hath He done unto them,
For He hath left them in the hands of them that prevailed.
He hath turned away His face from pitying them,
Young and old and their children together;
For they had done evil one and all, in not hearkening.
And the heavens were angry,
And the earth abhorred them;
For no man upon it had done what they did,

[5] Ps. 2: Psalms of Solomon, trans. G. Buchanan Gray, in Charles, vol. II, pp. 631 ff.

And the earth recognized all Thy righteous judgements, O God.
They set the sons of Jerusalem to be mocked at in return for the harlots in her;
Every wayfarer entered in in the full light of day.
They made mock with their transgressions, as they themselves were wont to do;
In the full light of day they revealed their iniquities.
And the daughters of Jerusalem were defiled in accordance with Thy judgement,
Because they had defiled themselves with unnatural intercourse.
I am pained in my bowels and my inward parts for these things.
And yet I will justify Thee, O God, in uprightness of heart,
For in Thy judgements is Thy righteousness displayed, O God.
For Thou hast rendered to the sinners according to their deeds,
Yea according to their sins, which were very wicked.
Thou hast uncovered their sins, that Thy judgement might be manifest;
Thou hast wiped out their memorial from the earth.
God is a righteous judge,
And He is no respecter of persons.
For the nations reproached Jerusalem, trampling it down;
Her beauty was dragged down from the throne of glory.
She girded on sackcloth instead of comely raiment,
A rope was about her head instead of a crown.
She put off the glorious diadem which God had set upon her,
In dishonour was her beauty cast upon the ground.
And I saw and entreated the Lord and said,
Long enough, O Lord, has Thine hand been heavy on Israel, in bringing the nations upon them.
For they have made sport unsparingly in wrath and fierce anger;
And they will make an utter end, unless Thou, O Lord, rebuke them in Thy wrath.
For they have done it not in zeal, but in lust of soul,
Pouring out their wrath upon us with a view to rapine.

Delay not, O God, to recompense them on their heads,
To turn the pride of the dragon into dishonour.
And I had not long to wait before God showed me the insolent one
Slain on the mountains of Egypt,
Esteemed of less account than the least, on land and sea;
His body, too, borne hither and thither on the billows with much insolence,
With none to bury him, because He had rejected him with dishonour.
He reflected not that he was man,
And reflected not on the latter end;
He said: I will be lord of land and sea;
And he recognized not that it is God who is great,
Mighty in His great strength.
He is king over the heavens,
And judgeth kings and kingdoms.
It is He who setteth me up in glory,
And bringeth down the proud to eternal destruction in dishonour,
Because they knew Him not.
And now behold, ye princes of the earth, the judgement of the Lord,
For a great king and righteous is He, judging all that is under heaven.
Bless God, ye that fear the Lord with wisdom,
For the mercy of the Lord will be upon them that fear Him, in the Judgement;
So that He will distinguish between the righteous and the sinner,
And recompense the sinners for ever according to their deeds;
And have mercy on the righteous, delivering him from the affliction of the sinner,
And recompensing the sinner for what he has done to the righteous.

For the Lord is good to them that call upon Him in patience,
Doing according to His mercy to His pious ones,
Establishing them at all times before Him in strength.
Blessed be the Lord for ever before His servants.

(Psalms of Solomon, 3; *ibid.*, p. 634)

Why sleepest thou, O my soul,
And blessest not the Lord?
Sing a new song,
Unto God who is worthy to be praised.
Sing and be wakeful
For good is a psalm sung to God from a glad heart.
The righteous remember the Lord at all times,
With thanksgiving and declaration of the righteousness of the Lord's judgements.
The righteous despiseth not the chastening of the Lord;
His will is always before the Lord;
The righteous stumbleth and holdeth the Lord righteous:
He falleth and looketh out for what God will do to him;
He seeketh out whence his deliverance will come.
The steadfastness of the righteous is from God their deliverer;
There lodgeth not in the house of the righteous sin upon sin.
The righteous continually searcheth his house,
To remove utterly all iniquity done by him in error.
He maketh atonement for sins of ignorance by fasting and afflicting his soul,
And the Lord counteth guiltless every pious man and his house.
The sinner stumbleth and curseth his life,
The day when he was begotten, and his mother's travail.
He addeth sins to sins, while he liveth;
He falleth—verily grievous is his fall—and riseth no more.
The destruction of the sinner is for ever,
And he shall not be remembered, when the righteous is visited.
This is the portion of sinners for ever.
But they that fear the Lord shall rise to life eternal,
And their life shall be in the light of the Lord, and shall come to an end no more.

(Psalms of Solomon, 5; *ibid.*, p. 637)

O Lord God, I will praise Thy name with joy,
In the midst of them that know Thy righteous judgements.
For Thou art good and merciful, the refuge of the poor;
When I cry to Thee, do not silently disregard me.
For no man taketh spoil from a mighty man;
Who, then, can take aught of all that Thou hast made, except Thou Thyself givest?
For man and his portion lie before Thee in the balance;
He cannot add to, so as to enlarge, what has been prescribed by Thee.
O God, when we are in distress we call upon Thee for help,
For Thou dost not turn back our petition, for Thou art our God.
Cause not Thy hand to be heavy upon us,
Lest through necessity we sin.
Even though Thou restore us not, we will not keep away;
But unto Thee will we come.
For if I hunger, unto Thee will I cry, O God;
And Thou wilt give to me.
Birds and fish dost Thou nourish,
In that Thou givest rain to the steppes that green grass may spring up,
So to prepare fodder in the steppes for every living thing;
And if they hunger, unto Thee do they lift up their face.
Kings and rulers and peoples Thou dost nourish, O God;
And who is the help of the poor and needy, if not Thou, O Lord?
And Thou wilt hearken—for who is good and gentle but Thou?—
Making glad the soul of the humble by opening Thine hand in mercy.
Man's goodness is bestowed grudgingly and at a price,
And if he repeat it without murmuring, even that is marvellous.
But Thy gift is great in goodness and wealth,
And he whose hope is set on Thee shall have no lack of gifts.
Upon the whole earth is Thy mercy, O Lord, in goodness.

Happy is he whom God remembereth in granting him a due sufficiency;
If a man abound overmuch, he sinneth.
Sufficient are moderate means with righteousness,
And hereby the blessing of the Lord becomes abundance with righteousness.
They that fear the Lord rejoice in good gifts,
And Thy goodness is upon Israel in Thy kingdom.
Blessed is the glory of the Lord, for He is our king.

(Psalms of Solomon, 7; *ibid.*, p. 639)

Make not Thy dwelling afar from us, O God;
Lest they assail us that hate us without cause.
For Thou hast rejected them, O God;
Let not their foot trample upon Thy holy inheritance.
Chasten us Thyself in Thy good pleasure;
But give us not up to the nations;
For, if Thou sendest pestilence,
Thou Thyself givest it charge concerning us;
For Thou art merciful,
And wilt not be angry to the point of consuming us.
While Thy name dwelleth in our midst, we shall find mercy;
And the nations shall not prevail against us.
For Thou art our shield,
And when we call upon Thee, Thou hearkenest to us;
For Thou wilt pity the seed of Israel for ever
And Thou wilt not reject them:
But we shall be under Thy yoke for ever,
And under the rod of Thy chastening.
Thou wilt establish us in the time that Thou helpest us,
Showing mercy to the house of Jacob on the day wherein Thou didst promise to help them.

(Psalms of Solomon, 9; *ibid.*, p. 642)

When Israel was led away captive into a strange land,
When they fell away from the Lord who redeemed them,
They were cast away from the inheritance, which the Lord had given them.

Among every nation were the dispersed of Israel according to the word of God,
That Thou mightest be justified, O God, in Thy righteousness by reason of our transgressions:
For Thou art a just judge over all the peoples of the earth.
For from Thy knowledge none that doeth unjustly is hidden,
And the righteous deeds of Thy pious ones are before Thee, O Lord;
Where, then, can a man hide himself from Thy knowledge, O God?
Our works are subject to our own choice and power
To do right or wrong in the works of our hands;
And in Thy righteousness Thou visitest the sons of men.
He that doeth righteousness layeth up life for himself with the Lord;
And he that doeth wrongly forfeits his life to destruction;
For the judgements of the Lord are given in righteousness to every man and his house.
Unto whom art Thou good, O God, except to them that call upon the Lord?
He cleanseth from sins a soul when it maketh confession, when it maketh acknowledgement;
For shame is upon us and upon our faces on account of all these things.
And to whom doth He forgive sins, except to them that have sinned?
Thou blessest the righteous, and dost not reprove them for the sins that they have committed;
And Thy goodness is upon them that sin, when they repent.
And, now, Thou art our God, and we the people whom Thou hast loved:
Behold and show pity, O God of Israel, for we are Thine;
And remove not Thy mercy from us, lest they assail us.
For Thou didst choose the seed of Abraham before all the nations,
And didst set Thy name upon us, O Lord,
And Thou wilt not reject us for ever.

Thou madest a covenant with our fathers concerning us;
And we hope in Thee, when our soul turneth unto Thee.
The mercy of the Lord will be upon the house of Israel for ever and ever.

(Psalms of Solomon, 17; *ibid.*, p. 647)

O Lord, Thou art our king for ever and ever,
For in Thee, O God, doth our soul glory.
How long are the days of man's life upon the earth?
As are his days, so is the hope set upon him.
But we hope in God, our deliverer;
For the might of our God is for ever with mercy,
And the kingdom of our God is for ever over the nations in judgement.
Thou, O Lord, didst choose David to be king over Israel,
And swaredst to him touching his seed that never should his kingdom fail before Thee.
But, for our sins, sinners rose up against us;
They assailed us and thrust us out;
What Thou hadst not promised to them, they took away from us with violence.
They in no wise glorified Thy honourable name;
They set a worldly monarchy in place of that which was their excellency;
They laid waste the throne of David in tumultuous arrogance.
But Thou, O God, didst cast them down, and remove their seed from the earth,
In that there rose up against them a man that was alien to our race.
According to their sins didst Thou recompense them, O God;
So that it befell them according to their deeds.
God showed them no pity;
He sought out their seed and let not one of them go free.
Faithful is the Lord in all His judgements
Which He doeth upon the earth.
The lawless one laid waste our land so that none inhabited it,
They destroyed young and old and their children together.

In the heat of His anger He sent them away even unto the west,
And He exposed the rulers of the land unsparingly to derision.
Being an alien the enemy acted proudly,
And his heart was alien from our God.
And all . . . Jerusalem,
As also the nations . . .
And the children of the covenant in the midst of the mingled peoples . . .
There was not among them one that wrought in the midst of Jerusalem mercy and truth.
They that loved the synagogues of the pious fled from them,
As sparrows that fly from their nest.
They wandered in deserts that their lives might be saved from harm,
And precious in the eyes of them that lived abroad was any that escaped alive from them.
Over the whole earth they were scattered by lawless men.
For the heavens withheld the rain from dropping upon the earth,
Springs were stopped that sprang perennially out of the deeps, that ran down from lofty mountains.
For there was none among them that wrought righteousness and justice;
From the chief of them to the least of them all were sinful;
The king was a transgressor, and the judge disobedient, and the people sinful.
Behold, O Lord, and raise up unto them their king, the son of David,
At the time in the which Thou seest, O God, that he may reign over Israel, Thy servant.
And gird him with strength, that he may shatter unrighteous rulers,
And that he may purge Jerusalem from nations that trample her down to destruction.
Wisely, righteously he shall thrust out sinners from the inheritance,
He shall destroy the pride of the sinner as a potter's vessel.

With a rod of iron he shall break in pieces all their substance,
He shall destroy the godless nations with the word of his mouth;
At his rebuke nations shall flee before him,
And he shall reprove sinners for the thoughts of their heart.
And he shall gather together a holy people, whom he shall lead in righteousness,
And he shall judge the tribes of the people that has been sanctified by the Lord his God.
And he shall not suffer unrighteousness to lodge any more in their midst,
Nor shall there dwell with them any man that knoweth wickedness,
For he shall know them, that they are all sons of their God.
And he shall divide them according to their tribes upon the land,
And neither sojourner nor alien shall sojourn with them any more.
He shall judge peoples and nations in the wisdom of his righteousness. *Selah.*
And he shall have the heathen nations to serve him under his yoke;
And he shall glorify the Lord in a place to be seen of all the earth;
And he shall purge Jerusalem, making it holy as of old:
So that nations shall come from the ends of the earth to see his glory,
Bringing as gifts her sons who had fainted,
And to see the glory of the Lord, wherewith God hath glorified her.
And he shall be a righteous king, taught of God, over them,
And there shall be no unrighteousness in his days in their midst,
For all shall be holy and their king the anointed of the Lord.
For he shall not put his trust in horse and rider and bow,
Nor shall he multiply for himself gold and silver for war,
Nor shall he gather confidence from a multitude for the day of battle.

The Lord Himself is his king, the hope of him that is mighty through his hope in God.
All nations shall be in fear before him,
For he will smite the earth with the word of his mouth for ever.
He will bless the people of the Lord with wisdom and gladness.
And he himself will be pure from sin, so that he may rule a great people.
He will rebuke rulers, and remove sinners by the might of his word;
And relying upon his God, throughout his days he will not stumble;
For God will make him mighty by means of His holy spirit,
And wise by means of the spirit of understanding, with strength and righteousness.
And the blessing of the Lord will be with him: he will be strong and stumble not;
His hope will be in the Lord: who then can prevail against him?
He will be mighty in his works, and strong in the fear of God,
He will be shepherding the flock of the Lord faithfully and righteously,
And will suffer none among them to stumble in their pasture.
He will lead them all aright,
And there will be no pride among them that any among them should be oppressed.
This will be the majesty of the king of Israel whom God knoweth;
He will raise him up over the house of Israel to correct him.
His words shall be more refined than costly gold, the choicest;
In the assemblies he will judge the peoples, the tribes of the sanctified.
His words shall be like the words of the holy ones in the midst of sanctified peoples.
Blessed be they that shall be in those days,
In that they shall see the good fortune of Israel which God shall bring to pass in the gathering together of the tribes.

May the Lord hasten His mercy upon Israel!
May He deliver us from the uncleanness of unholy enemies!
The Lord Himself is our king for ever and ever.

But this wholly instinctive reaction gave place to a more intellectual reflection. After such unprecedented woes we see developing in various different quarters a sort of theology of history, using these terms in a very general way. It seemed reasonable, for example, to relate the dreadful times Israel was living through to the days foretold by Isaias (c. 24):

> Look you, the Lord means to make earth a void, a wilderness; twist it out of shape, and scatter its inhabitants far and wide. One law for priest and people, for master and servant, for mistress and maid; for seller and buyer, for borrower and lender, for debtor and exactor of debts. Earth drained to its dregs, earth ravaged and ransacked; such decree the Lord has uttered. Earth woebegone and withered, a world that withers and grows feeble; how feeble they have grown now, the great ones of the earth! Poor earth, polluted by the men that dwell on it; they have broken God's law, traversed the decree he made for them, violated his eternal covenant with men; cankered it lies by a curse, peopled with guilty men, only a frantic remnant left of its inhabitants. Woebegone the vintage, withered now the vine, hearts sighing that once were merry; silent the gay tambour, hushed the noise of holiday-making, silent the harp's mirth. No more feasting and song; the wine turns bitter in their mouths. Ransacked and ruined lies yonder city, where every house denies entrance, and a cry goes up in the streets because all the wine is spent, the mirth forsaken, the joy vanished; a city left to desolation, with ruin fallen upon its gates.
>
> In the midst of the wide earth, among those many peoples, what shall be left? A remnant, the last olives that are shaken from the tree, the gleanings that remain when vintage-time is over. Few only, but they shall lift up their voices in praise; God's honour vindicated, their rejoicing shall be heard across the sea, Give glory to God, where knowledge of him is revealed; praise to the God of Israel among the distant isles; here

at the ends of the earth his song of triumph has reached us, the boast of his elect. Heart, keep thy secret, heart, keep thy secret; no more of that.

But alas, the traitors still betray his cause; treachery is treachery still, and its fruit is treason. For the dwellers on earth, tidings of fear; pit and snare await them; flee they from tidings of fear, they shall fall into the pit, flee they from the pit, they shall be held fast in the snare. The flood-gates of heaven will be opened, and the foundations of earth rock; earth must be rent and riven, earth torn and tattered, earth must quiver and quake; earth rolling and reeling like a drunkard, earth tottering like some frail shelter that is gone in a night, bowed down by the weight of its own guilt, till it falls, never to rise again. When that day comes, the Lord will hold a reckoning with the hosts of heaven, there above, with the kings of the earth, here on earth; huddled together, as captives are huddled together in a dungeon, they shall remain prisoners; so, at last, the reckoning will be held. And then the Lord of hosts will reign at Jerusalem, on Mount Sion; and the moon will be put to shame, and the sun hide his face, before the glory in which he will appear then, with the elders of his people about him.

Surely the measure was filled to overflowing; the sins of the wicked surpassed what could be borne, and already the "day of the Lord" was at hand. This feeling produced a great flowering of apocalyptic literature. Hardly a single work does not contain "revelations" of the end of the world and the judgement of God and the New Jerusalem. "Predictions" about "the day of the Beast", in which wickedness, having broken all bounds, will call down the wrath of God, are generally transposed into an esoteric language describing the events of the writer's own time. This frequently makes it possible to date the man who is hidden behind the name of Esdras or Enoch, Moses or Baruch.

Before we quote any texts, it will be as well to glance at the eschatology, the ideas of the end of the world, presented in the Old Testament and rabbinical teaching.

If the laws of God implanted in nature are immutable, as the Psalmist says:

> Praise him, sun and moon; praise him, every star that shines. Praise him, you highest heavens, you waters beyond the heavens. Let all these praise the Lord; it was his command that created them. He has set them there unageing for ever, given them a law that cannot be altered. (Ps. 148. 3–6)
> The earth thou hast planted on its own firm base, undisturbed for all time. (Ps. 103. 5)

Yet the world is not eternal:

> It was thou, Lord, that didst lay the foundations of the earth when time began, it was thy hand that built the heavens. They will perish, but thou wilt remain; they will all be like a cloak that grows threadbare, and thou wilt lay them aside like a garment, and exchange them for new. (Ps. 101. 26–27)

Time ceases: it is the day of Judgement.

It is difficult to see what is the precise teaching on the question whether the day of the Lord will end the reign of the ungodly and open the age of the new, reborn Jerusalem and of the Messias, or whether, as in traditional Catholic theology, it will mark the end of the visible world. In any case, for the writers of the apocrypha, it is certainly regarded as a manifestation of the Lord which will sweep the ungodly from before his face, and will establish a restored Jerusalem. For now, Israel is oppressed, and it is the reign of the Beast:[6]

> And it came to pass the second night that I saw a dream: and lo! there came up from the sea an eagle which had twelve feathered wings, and three heads. And I beheld, and lo! he spread his wings over the whole earth, and all the winds of heaven blew on him, and the clouds were gathered together unto him. And I beheld, and lo! out of his wings there grew anti-wings; and they became wings petty and small. But his heads were at rest; the middle head was greater than the other

[6] 4 Ezra, trans. G. H. Box, in Charles, vol. II, pp. 609 ff.

heads, yet it rested with them. And I beheld, and lo! the eagle flew with his wings to reign over the earth and over them that dwell therein. And I beheld how all things under heaven were subject unto him, and no-one spoke against him—not even one of the creatures upon earth. And I beheld and lo! the eagle rose upon his talons, and uttered his voice to his wings, saying, Watch not all at once: sleep every one in his place, and watch by course: but let the heads be preserved for the last. And I beheld, and lo! the voice proceeded not from his heads, but from the midst of his body. And I numbered his anti-wings, and lo! there were eight.

And I beheld, and lo! there arose one wing, and reigned over the whole earth. And it came to pass that, after it had reigned, it came to its end and disappeared, so that the place of it was not visible. Then arose the second and reigned, and this bare rule for a long time. And it came to pass that, after it had reigned, it also came to its end, so that it disappeared even as the first. And lo! a voice sounded which said to it: Hear, thou that hast borne rule over the earth so long a time: this I proclaim unto thee before thou shalt disappear—After thee shall none bear rule the length of thy time, nay not even the half of it! Then the third lifted itself up and held the rule even as the former, and it also disappeared. And so it fell to all the wings to rule and then disappear. And I beheld, and lo! in process of time the little wings also were set up that they also might hold the rule; and some of them bare rule but disappeared suddenly: and some of them were set up but did not hold the rule. After this I beheld, and lo! the twelve wings disappeared, and two little wings; and nothing was left in the eagle's body save only the three heads that were at rest, and six little wings. And I beheld, and lo! from the six little wings two detached themselves, and remained under the head that was upon the right side: but four remained in their place. And I beheld, and lo! these under-wings thought to set themselves up and to hold the rule. And I beheld, and lo! one was set up, but immediately disappeared; a second also, and this disappeared more quickly than the first. And I beheld, and lo! the two that remained thought also in themselves to reign; and while they were thinking thus, lo! one of the heads that were at rest—it, namely, that was in the midst—awoke; for this one was greater than the two other heads. And I beheld how it allied with itself the two other heads; and lo! the head was turned with them that were with it, and did eat up the two under-wings that thought to have reigned. This head bare rule over the whole earth, and exercised lordship over the dwellers therein with much oppression; and it wielded more power over the inhabited world than all the wings that had been. And after this I beheld, and lo! the middle head suddenly disappeared, even as the wings. But there remained the two heads which also reigned over the earth, and over the inhabitants therein. And I beheld, and lo! the head upon the right side devoured that which was upon the left. Then I heard a voice, which said unto me: Look before thee, and consider what thou seest. And I beheld, and lo! as it were a lion, roused out of the wood, roaring; and I heard how he uttered a man's voice against the eagle; and he spake, saying: Hear, thou Eagle—I will talk with thee; the Most High saith to thee: Art thou not it that remainest of the four beasts which I made to reign in my world, that the end of my times might come through them? Thou, however, the fourth, who art come, hast overcome all the beasts that are past;

Thou hast wielded power over the world with great terror,
  and over all the inhabited earth with grievous oppression;
Thou hast dwelt so long in the civilized world with fraud,
  and hast judged the earth, but not with faithfulness:
For thou hast afflicted the meek,
  and oppressed the peaceable;
Thou hast hated the upright,
  and loved liars;
Thou hast destroyed the strongholds of the fruitful,
  and laid low the walls of such as did thee no harm—
And so thine insolence hath ascended to the Most High,
  and thy pride to the Mighty One.
Then the Most High regarded his times—
  and lo! they were ended;
And his ages—
  and they were fulfilled.

Therefore shalt thou disappear, O thou Eagle,
and thy horrible wings,
and thy little wings most evil,
thy harm-dealing heads,
thy hurtful talons,
and all thy worthless body!

And so the whole earth, freed from thy violence, shall be refreshed again, and hope for the judgement and mercy of him that made her.

And it came to pass, while the lion spake these words unto the eagle, I beheld, and lo! the head that remained disappeared. And the two wings, which went over unto it, set themselves up to reign; and their rule was short and full of uproar. And I beheld, and lo! these also disappeared, and the whole body of the eagle was burnt; and the earth was terrified greatly.

This is the interpretation of the vision which thou hast seen. The eagle which thou sawest come up from the sea is the fourth kingdom which appeared in vision to thy brother Daniel. Behold, the days come when there shall arise a kingdom upon the earth, and it shall be more terrible than all the kingdoms that were before it. In it twelve kings shall reign, one after the other; and the second that shall reign, he shall bear rule a longer time than any of the twelve. This is the interpretation of the twelve wings which thou didst see. And whereas thou didst hear a voice which spake, going out not from his heads, but from the midst of his body, this is the interpretation: In the midst of the time of that kingdom there shall arise no small contentions, and it shall stand in peril of falling; nevertheless it shall not then fall, but shall be restored again to rule. And whereas thou didst see eight under-wings grow up with his wings, this is the interpretation: In it there shall arise eight kings, whose times shall be transient and years swift: and two of them shall perish when the middle time of the kingdom approaches; and four shall be kept for the time when its time for dissolution shall approach: but two shall be kept for the end. And whereas thou didst see three heads resting, this is the interpretation: In the last days thereof the Most High will raise up three kings; and they shall renew many things therein, and shall exercise lordship over the earth and over the dwellers therein with much oppression, above all those that were before them. Therefore are they called the heads of the eagle: for these are they that shall bring to a head his wickedness, and consummate his last end. And whereas thou didst see that the great head disappeared—one of them shall die upon his bed, but yet with pain. But as for the two who remain the sword shall devour them. For the sword of the one shall devour him that was with him; nevertheless this one also shall fall by the sword in the last days. And whereas thou didst see two under-wings passing over to the head that is upon the right side, this is the interpretation: These are they whom the Most High hath kept for his (i.e. the eagle's) end; and their rule shall be short and full of uproar, as thou hast seen. And as for the lion whom thou didst see roused from the wood and roaring, and speaking to the eagle and reproving him for his unrighteousness and all his deeds, as thou hast heard; this is the Messiah whom the Most High hath kept unto the end of the days, who shall spring from the seed of David, and shall come and speak unto them;

he shall reprove them for their ungodliness,
rebuke them for their unrighteousness,
reproach them to their face with their treacheries.

For at the first he shall set them alive for judgement; and when he hath rebuked them he shall destroy them.

But such dreadful times shall come upon the oppressors also:

Go now and announce to my people the foretellings that I shall put into thy mouth, said the Lord; and write them with care into a book, for they are sure and true. Fear not the plots they may contrive against thee, nor trouble thyself if they contradict thy words out of their unbelief, for every unbeliever shall die in his unbelief.

Evils shall spread over the earth, said the Lord: War, famine, death and destruction shall be the ministers of my vengeance. For all the earth is stained with their wrong-doing, and the cup of wickedness of those who inhabit the earth is filled to overflowing. For this reason, said the Lord,

I shall avenge myself on them for the impiety they commit against me in their ungodliness,
I shall suffer their wrong-doing and injustice no longer;
The blood of innocent men cries out to me,
and the souls of the just unceasingly call for vengeance.
I shall take a terrible vengeance, said the Lord,
and the impious shall render their account to me for the innocent blood they have shed.
My people have been led to death like a helpless flock;

I shall suffer them to remain in Egypt no longer. I shall lead them out of Egypt with a strong hand and my arm outstretched; I shall strike the land with new plagues, and shall ravage the length and breadth of the land. She shall be afflicted even to her foundations with the evils with which the Lord shall strike her. Her workmen shall weep, for blight and frost and evil things shall ravage their harvests. Cursed be the time and those who live in it!

The sword is lifted up against their head, and with the sword shall they soon be struck down. Their peoples shall make war one against another, already their weapons gleam in their hands. And in the midst of all these troubles there shall arise everywhere rebellions; no longer shall they recognize their legitimate kings, and their might shall be the only rule of action for their princes.

Those who would enter the city shall not be able to. Their cities shall be in confusion on account of the pride of those who inhabit them; their homes shall disappear under the ruins, and men shall be stricken with terror. They shall have no compassion one for another, and in the excess of their evils and their hunger they shall go abroad sword in hand to pillage and plunder.

These are my times, said the Lord, when I shall gather together all the kings of the east and the south and the north and of Lebanon, to strike terror into them, and to render unto them all the evils Israel has suffered at their hands. For I shall deal with them as they have dealt with my chosen people until this day. Thus the Lord spake, saying:

My arm shall be heavy upon the sinners,
nor shall my sword spare those who have stained the earth with the blood of innocent men,
But its anger shall spread like fire, and consume the earth to its foundations,
and the sinners shall become like unto burnt chaff.
Cursed be those who sin and obey not my commandments, said the Lord,
Never shall they obtain my forgiveness.

But you who are my children, keep yourselves apart from the impious, and do not you like them profane the sanctity of my name. For the Lord knows those who offend against him: those shall he deliver to death and to destruction. Already these evils are spread over the earth; you shall suffer them all, and the Lord shall not protect you, for you have offended against him.

In that time, terrible things shall be seen, and they shall begin to come from the east. Out of Arabia shall come hosts of dragons with their chariots, and they shall spread over the earth with the swiftness of the wind; at the noise of their coming, all men shall be seized with fear and trembling. The peoples of Carmos shall rise up in their anger, and go forth rashly against them, like wild boars rushing from the forests; they shall go forth to do battle with them, and shall ravage part of Assyria. But the dragons shall then recall the greatness of their rising, and gather themselves together to pursue them. Then trouble shall come upon those peoples; not daring to come against such might, they shall seek safety in flight. A warrior shall attack them in Assyria, and the fall of one of their own warriors shall spread terror throughout their army and cause division amongst their leaders.

Then clouds shall form from the east and the north even unto the south; dreadful clouds that shall spread everywhere the terrors of the storm. In their strife one with another they shall bring down a great number of stars, and among them the star that was foretold that they bear themselves. And in the destruction and slaughter that shall follow, men shall wade up to the waist in blood. And the rottenness of their corpses shall rise as high as the camels' girths: all the earth shall be in uproar. Those who shall see this day of wrath shall be seized with terror, and fear shall take hold of their minds.

Then shall there come clouds from the south and from the north, and others shall appear from the west. But the winds that arise from the east shall scatter these clouds, as well as the cloud that carries with it the storm, and the star which should put to flight the winds of the east and west shall be obscured. Then shall these great clouds arise in their strength and their anger and, followed by the star, shall spread terror over all the earth and over all those who dwell therein, and shall spread that deadly star over all the high places of the world. And from within the star shall come forth fire and hail and swift swords and torrents of water which shall swell the rivers so that they shall flood every country. And they shall overturn cities with their walls, and drag with them mountains and hills and forests and all the fruits of the earth.

Nothing shall hinder them, and they shall carry their destruction even unto Babylon. Up to her walls they shall come and surround them, and shall spread over that city the star and all the fury and malice that it contains: and at once shall the sky be darkened by the dust and the smoke that shall arise from the ruins; the peoples which dwell about Babylon shall bewail her fall. And those that remain within her walls shall fall under the domination of the conquerors.

And thou, Asia, who hast placed all thy hopes in Babylon, and madest of her the first city of thy empire and gavest her the glory, cursed be thou also, for that thou hast imitated her, and hast charmed thy daughters into sin, so that they might please those that loved them, and boast of their numbers, amongst those who have never ceased to burn with a sinful love for thee! Thou hast imitated that abominable city in all its works and in all its profligate sinfulness; and on account of this, said the Lord,

Every evil shall I send against thee: widowhood and poverty,
    famine, sword and plague,
  so that thy houses shall be destroyed with dishonour, with
    death and with the passing of thy power.
Thy glory shall wither like a flower,
  when the fire that is to consume thee shall appear.

And the great ones of the earth who loved thee so distractedly shall no longer have to do with thee,
when they see thee like unto one of those women whom poverty exposes to scorn and insult.
Would I thus have dealt with thee in my wrath,
Hadst thou not cruelly sacrificed my chosen people,
and ever drunk with their blood outraged these innocent men?
Gather then to thyself all those charms that thou mightest have,
for thou art going to receive the recompense for all thy shameful disorders;
As thou hast dealt with my chosen people, said the Lord,
so shall I deal with thee, and heap evils upon thee:
Thy children shall perish with hunger, and thou shalt perish by the sword,
Thy cities shall be destroyed,
Those of thy peoples who dwell in the country shall fall beneath the sword,
Those that flee to the mountains shall die of hunger,
And to such a pass shall they be brought by hunger and thirst that they shall eat their own flesh and drink their own blood.
From these horrors thou shalt seek a refuge beyond the sea,
but thou shalt flee only to new horrors.
Thine enemies shall fall upon thee,
They shall crush thee again and again,
They shall ravage thine empire
And destroy a part of thy glory
And return to Babylon;
And when they have destroyed thee, thou shalt serve them to light their fires,
And they shall swallow thee up, thee and thy cities and thy provinces and thy mountains,
They shall set fire upon thy forests and all thy fruit trees,
They shall lead thy children into captivity,
They shall plunder all thy wealth,
And they shall utterly destroy all thy beauty.

And it will be the day of the Lord:[7]

Concerning the signs, however:

Behold, the days come when the inhabitants of the earth shall
be seized with great panic,
And the way of truth shall be hidden,
and the land be barren of faith.

And iniquity shall be increased above that which thou thyself now seest or that thou hast heard of long ago. And the land that thou seest now to bear rule shall be a pathless waste; and men shall see it forsaken: if the Most High grant thee to live, thou shalt see it after the third period in confusion.

Then shall the sun suddenly shine forth by night
and the moon by day:
And blood shall trickle forth from wood,
and the stone utter its voice:
The peoples shall be in commotion,
the outgoings of the stars shall change.

And one whom the dwellers upon earth do not look for shall wield sovereignty, and the birds shall take to general flight, and the sea shall cast forth its fish.

And one whom the many do not know will make his voice heard by night; and all shall hear his voice.

And the earth o'er wide regions shall open,
and fire burst forth for a long period:

The wild beasts shall desert their haunts, and women bear monsters. Salt waters shall be found in the sweet; friends shall attack one another suddenly.

Then shall intelligence hide itself,
and wisdom withdraw to its chamber—
by many shall be sought and not found.

And unrighteousness and incontinency shall be multiplied upon the earth. One land shall also ask another and say: Is Righteousness—that doeth the right—passed through thee? And it shall answer, No.

[7] 4 Ezra, *loc. cit.*, pp. 569 ff.

And it shall be
In that time men shall hope and not obtain,
shall labour and not prosper.

Such are the signs I am permitted to tell thee; but if thou wilt pray again, and weep as now, and fast seven days, thou shalt hear again greater things than these.

I answered and said: O Lord my Lord, if I have found favour in thy sight, I beseech thee that thou show thy servant the last of thy signs of which thou didst show me a part in the night that is past.

And he answered and said unto me: Stand up upon thy feet, and thou shalt hear a voice exceeding loud; and it shall be if the place whereon thou standest be greatly shaken when it (i.e. the voice) speaks with thee, be not thou terrified; for the word is of the End, and the foundations of the earth shall understand that the speech is concerning themselves. They shall tremble and be shaken, for they know that their end is to be changed.

And it happened that when I had heard it I stood up upon my feet, and hearkened: and lo! a voice spake, and the sound of it was as the sound of mighty waters.

And it said:

Behold the days come, and it shall be,
When I am about to draw nigh
to visit the dwellers upon earth,
And when I require from the doers of iniquity
the penalty of their iniquity;
And when the humiliation of Sion
shall be complete,
And when the Age which is about to pass away
shall be sealed

then will I show these signs: the books shall be opened before the face of the firmament, and all see together.

And one-year-old children shall speak with their voices; pregnant women shall bring forth untimely births at three or four months, and these shall live and dance. And suddenly shall the sown places appear unsown, and the full storehouses shall suddenly be found empty.

And the trumpet shall sound aloud, at which all men, when they hear it, shall be struck with sudden fear. And at that time friends shall war against friends like enemies, the earth shall be stricken with fear together with the dwellers thereon, and the springs of the fountains shall stand still so that for three hours they shall not run.

And it shall be whosoever shall have survived all these things that I have foretold unto thee, he shall be saved and shall see my salvation and the end of my world. And the men who have been taken up, who have not tasted death from their birth, shall appear. Then shall the heart of the inhabitants of the world be changed, and converted to a different spirit.

For evil shall be blotted out,
and deceit extinguished;
Faithfulness shall flourish,
and corruption be vanquished;

And truth, which for so long a time has been without fruit, shall be made manifest.

And then shall come a new day for Sion, and "in that time the Lord will heal his servants, and they shall stand and see a great peace, and rout their enemies", and take possession of all the earth and hold it for ever.

Sure as they were that one day the Lord would avenge them, that they would become kings and lords over all the earth, the Jews were ready to suffer all persecutions, and yet remain faithful despite it all.

But more and more, this attitude made them strangers to the world.

CHAPTER V

THE QUMRAN COMMUNITY

It has been possible to discern in the apocryphal literature, which was all that was known until recently, some of the directions taken by Israel's resistance in the midst of all kinds of constraints and persecutions. But seventeen years ago there was restored to our knowledge, with an astonishing immediacy and vividness, one of those communities of pious Jews, one of those "small survivals" of Israel, which regarded itself as quite specially chosen to preserve, amid the apostasy of the majority, faithfulness to the covenant established between the Lord and Abraham, the father of the faithful. The history of the recovery of the Dead Sea Scrolls, and hence of the community of Qumran, is too well known to need long exposition here.

In 1947, nomadic Bedouins found in a cave above the Dead Sea some jars containing manuscripts. These they offered without success to a Muslim antiquarian in Bethlehem, but they found someone willing to buy them in the Syrian Metropolitan of Jerusalem. He was at first discouraged by the specialists he consulted, but then the acting Director of the American School of Oriental Research, Dr John C. Trever, quickly perceived the antiquity and the value of the manuscripts. During the same period, the late Dr E. L. Sukenik,

Professor of Archaeology at the Hebrew University, had come into possession of a number of other documents which had been found in the same way.

All this was in the middle of a war. The United Nations Organization had just established the State of Israel, and bloody battles were being fought between Arabs and Israelis. As a result, no serious archaeological expedition was possible for two years, and the cave was open to any that went to dig in secret. When the archaeologists were at last able, at the beginning of 1949, to get into the cave, they found only Roman or Hellenistic potsherds, some linen cloths which had been wrapped round the rolled manuscripts and tiny fragments of manuscripts of canonical and apocryphal books. Despite the paucity of the evidence, it showed clearly that this had been the hiding-place of an important library, and that the manuscripts (some of which were of much greater antiquity) had been hidden there in the first century A.D. It was also clear, as much from the number of broken pots as from the manuscript fragments, that what was found by the Bedouin in 1947 was only a small part of the original deposit. The hiding-place had therefore been despoiled before: and it was then remembered that Origen, in the third century, had mentioned Greek and Hebrew books being found in a jar near Jericho; that the Nestorian patriarch Timotheus had spoken in the ninth century of the recent finding of Hebrew manuscripts in a cave in the same region; and that a Jewish sect, the Qaraites, claimed as their authorities the "men of the cave", so called because their scriptures had been found in a cave.

Who, then, hid these manuscripts in the jars in the cave?

Less than a mile to the south of the cave stand the ruins of Khirbet Qumran, where no systematic excavation had ever been carried out. Perhaps these ruins contained the key? The result was as it were the resurrection of an important Essene community which had fled before the Roman advance (*c.* A.D. 68) during the Jewish War, and hid its most precious treasures, its scriptures, in almost inaccessible caves. Fruitful excavation continued—and continues—in the same region.

Before we examine more closely the documents and the life of that Essene community, we give a list of the most important finds. Their antiquity and origins are corroborated by the vast number of objects of daily life and of coins found in the same area.

The Old Testament:

Isaias—complete in Hebrew
Isaias—incomplete in Hebrew

Fragments in Hebrew of:

Genesis
Exodus
Leviticus
Numbers
Deuteronomy
Judges
Samuel
Isaias
Jeremias
Psalms
Ruth
Daniel
Tobias

Fragments in Aramaic:

Daniel
Tobias

Fragments in Greek:

Minor Prophets
Wisdom

Fragments in Syriac:

Josue

The New Testament:

Fragments in Greek:

Mark
John
Acts of the Apostles

Fragments in Syriac:

Matthew
Luke
Acts of the Apostles
Epistle to the Colossians

Non-canonical texts:

Fragments in Hebrew:

Book of Jubilees
Book of Enoch
Unknown apocrypha

Fragments in Aramaic:

The Apocalypse of Lamech

Texts peculiar to the Qumran community:

Commentary on Habacuc
Rules of the Community in Hebrew
The War of the Sons of Light and the Sons of Darkness
Hymns

Fragments in Hebrew:

Commentary on Michaeas
Commentary of Ps. 37 (36)
Commentary on Isaias
Formulary of blessings
The Damascus documents
Some copper leaves

and various other documents—letters, contracts, etc.—in Hebrew, Aramaic and Greek.

What has the Qumran community to do with our theme? What have these pious Jews, who took refuge in the desert, to do with the Old Testament apocrypha?

The list of works shows that they used, beside the canonical books of the Bible, both the apocrypha we already know and their own books, both filling in the "gaps", the "silences", of the Scriptures.

Without going too far into the archaeological and historical substructures on which they are built (details of which can be found in some of the books mentioned in the bibliography), we give here briefly the more or less unanimous conclusions reached concerning this Essene community.

We have seen that the spiritual sons of the Chasidim were the Pharisees, who, after some unpleasant experiences, had withdrawn from political life. It seems likely, though there is no certain documentary evidence to prove it, that as the observance of the law in its integrity became more and more difficult, a schism was produced, and the extreme rigorists thought it their duty to retire to the desert. The first settlement at Qumran dates from 110 B.C., a time when the Jews were divided into factions—the pro-Egyptians, the pro-Syrians and the nationalists behind the descendants of the Machabees. Leaving aside a small faction of Hellenistic Jews, these pious Jews themselves were not united: some thought that only national independence could make possible the full observance of the law, and very often their nationalism was stronger than their faith. Others believed that a liberal foreign domination could assure them of the political protection needed for a true religious way of life. Nor were these purely intellectual choices: civil war, more or less endemic, was added to the war with the foreigners, while the conquerors, relying first on one party and then on another, did not hesitate to turn their arms against their friends of yesterday in order to show their good faith to their friends of today.

In one way and another the peace and stability indispensable for a truly religious life became less than possible in the great cities. It was natural enough that pious men should get together to build a community sheltered from the insecurity and unrest about them. The same thing happened several centuries later, when the monastic orders flourished at the time of the great invasions, in the east and in the west.

What do we know about the Qumran community, and how do we know? First, we know their rule perfectly, and their way of life, partly through the documents which have been found, and were previously unknown, and partly by a text known before, the Zadokite Document, on which a new light has been thrown by its resemblances to the rule of the community and by the fact that it was part of the Essenes' library. Let the texts speak, to tell us of the spirit of the Essenes:[1]

The Aim and Rule of the Community

> Everyone who wishes to join the community must pledge himself to respect God and man; to live according to the communal rule; to seek God [...]; to do what is good and upright in His sight, in accordance with what He has commanded through Moses and through His servants the prophets; to love all that He has chosen and hate all that He has rejected; to keep far from all evil and to cling to all good works; to act truthfully and righteously and justly on earth and to walk no more in the stubbornness of a guilty heart and of lustful eyes, doing all manner of evil; to bring into a bond of mutual love all who have declared their willingness to carry out the statutes of God; to join the formal community of God; to walk blamelessly before Him in conformity with His various laws and dispositions; to love all the children of light, each according to his stake in the formal community of God; and to hate all the children of darkness, each according to the measure of his guilt, which God will ultimately requite.

[1] Translations from *The Scriptures of the Dead Sea Sect*, Translation, Introduction and Notes by Theodore H. Gaster; London, Secker and Warburg, and New York, Doubleday, 1957.

All who declare their willingness to serve God's truth must bring all their mind, all of their strength, and all of their wealth into the community of God, so that their minds may be purified by the truth of His precepts, their strength controlled by His perfect ways, and their wealth disposed in accordance with His just design. They must not deviate by a single step from carrying out the orders of God at the times appointed for them; they must neither advance the statutory times nor postpone the prescribed seasons. They must not turn aside from the ordinances of God's truth either to the right or to the left.

Moreover, all who would join the ranks of the community must enter into a covenant in the presence of God to do according to all that He has commanded and not to turn away from Him through any fear or terror or through any trial to which they may be subjected through the domination of Belial.

When they enter into that covenant, the priests and the levites are to pronounce a blessing upon the God of salvation and upon all that He does to make known His truth; and all that enter the covenant are to say after them, Amen, amen.

Then the priests are to rehearse the bounteous acts of God as revealed in all His deeds of power, and they are to recite all His tender mercies towards Israel; while the levites are to rehearse the iniquities of the children of Israel and all the guilty transgressions and sins that they have committed through the domination of Belial. And all who enter the covenant are to make confession after them, saying, We have acted perversely, we have transgressed, we have sinned, we have done wickedly, ourselves and our fathers before us, in that we have gone counter to the truth. God has been right to bring His judgement upon us and upon our fathers. Howbeit, always from ancient times He has also bestowed His mercies upon us, and so will He do for all time to come.

Then the priests are to invoke a blessing on all that have cast their lot with God, that walk blamelessly in all their ways; and they are to say: May He bless thee with all good and keep thee from all evil, and illumine thy heart with insight into the things of life, and grace thee with knowledge of things eternal, and lift up His gracious countenance towards thee to grant thee peace everlasting.

The levites, on the other hand, are to invoke a curse on all that have cast their lot with Belial, and to say in response: Cursed art thou for all thy wicked guilty works. May God make thee a thing of abhorrence at the hands of all who would wreak vengeance, and visit thine offspring with destruction at the hands of all who would mete out retribution. Cursed art thou, beyond hope of mercy. Even as thy works are wrought in darkness, so mayest thou be damned in the gloom of the fire eternal. May God show thee no favour when thou callest, neither pardon nor forgive thine iniquities. May He lift up an angry countenance towards thee, to wreak vengeance upon thee. May no man wish thee peace of all that truly claim their patrimony.

And all that enter the covenant shall say alike after them that bless and after them that curse, Amen, amen.

Thereupon the priests and the levites shall continue and say: Cursed be everyone that has come to enter this covenant with the taint of idolatry in his heart and who hath set his iniquity as a stumbling-block before him so that thereby he may defect, and who, when he hears the terms of this covenant, blesses himself in his heart, saying, May it go well with me, for I shall go on walking in the stubbornness of my heart! Whether he satisfy his passions or whether he still thirst for their fulfilment, his spirit shall be swept away and receive no pardon. The anger of God and the fury of His judgements shall consume him as by fire unto his eternal extinction, and there shall cleave unto him all the curses threatened in this covenant. God shall set him apart for misfortune, and he shall be cut off from the midst of all the children of light in that through the taint of his idolatry and through the stumbling-block of his iniquity he has defected from God. God will set his lot among those that are accursed for ever! And all who have been admitted to the covenant shall say after them in response, Amen, amen.

The following procedure is to be followed year by year so long as Belial continues to hold sway.

The priests are first to be reviewed in due order, one after another, in respect of the state of their spirits. After them, the levites shall be similarly reviewed, and in the third place all the laity one after another, in their thousands, hundreds, fifties and tens. The object is that every man in Israel may be made aware of his status in the community of God in the sense of the ideal, eternal society, and that none may be abased below his status, nor exalted above his allotted place. All of them will thus be members of a community founded at once upon true values and upon a becoming sense of humility, upon charity and mutual fairness—members of a society truly hallowed, partners in an everlasting communion.

Anyone who refuses to enter the ideal society of God and persists in walking in the stubbornness of his heart shall not be admitted to this community of God's truth. For in as much as his soul has revolted at the discipline entailed in a knowledge of God's righteous judgements, he has shown no real strength in amending his way of life, and therefore cannot be reckoned with the upright. The mental, physical and material resources of such a man are not to be introduced into the stock of the community, for such a man "plows in the slime of wickedness" and "there are stains on his repentance". He is not honest in resolving the stubbornness of his heart. On paths of light he sees but darkness. Such a man cannot be reckoned as among those essentially blameless. He cannot be cleared by mere ceremonies of atonement, nor cleansed by any waters of ablution, nor sanctified by immersion in lakes or in rivers, nor purified by any bath. Unclean, unclean he remains so long as he rejects the government of God and refuses the discipline of communion with Him. For it is only through the spiritual apprehension of God's truth that man's ways can be properly directed. Only thus can all his iniquities be shriven so that he can gaze upon the true light of life. Only through the holy spirit can he achieve union with God's truth and be purged of all his iniquities. Only by a spirit of uprightness and humility can his sin be atoned. Only by the submission of his soul to all the ordinances of God can his flesh be made clean. Only thus can it really be sprinkled with waters of ablution. Only thus can it really be sanctified by waters of purification. And only thus can he really direct his steps to walk blamelessly through all the vicissitudes of his destiny in all the ways of God in the manner which He has commanded, without turning either to the right or to the left and without overstepping any of God's words. Then indeed will he be acceptable before God like an atonement-offering which meets with His pleasure, and then indeed will he be admitted to the covenant of the community for ever.

This is for the man who would bring others to the inner vision, so that he may understand and teach to all the children of light the real nature of men, touching the different varieties of their temperaments with the distinguishing traits thereof, touching their actions throughout their generations, and touching the reason why they are now visited with afflictions and now enjoy periods of well-being.

All that is and ever was comes from a God of knowledge. Before things came into existence He determined the plan of them; and when they fill their appointed rôles, it is in accordance with His glorious design that they discharge their functions. Nothing can be changed. In His hand lies the government of all things. God it is that sustains them in their needs.

Now, this God created man to rule the world, and appointed for him two spirits after whose direction he was to walk until the final Inquisition. They are the spirits of truth and of perversity.

The origin of truth lies in the Fountain of Light, and that of perversity in the Wellspring of Darkness. All who practise righteousness are under the domination of the Prince of Lights, and walk in the ways of light; whereas all who practise perversity are under the domination of the Angel of Darkness and walk in the ways of darkness. Through the Angel of Darkness, however, even those who practise righteousness are made liable to error. All their sin and their iniquities, all their guilt and their deeds of transgression are the result of his domination; and this, by God's inscrutable design, will continue until the time appointed by Him. Moreover, all men's afflictions and all their moments of tribulation are due to this being's malevolent sway. All of the spirits that attend upon him are bent on causing the sons of light to stumble. Howbeit, the God of Israel and the Angel of His truth are always there to help the sons of light. It is God that created these spirits of light and darkness and made them the basis of every act, the [instigators] of every deed and the directors of every thought. The one He loves to all eternity, and is ever pleased with its deeds; but any association with the other He abhors, and He hates all its ways to the end of time.

This is the way those spirits operate in the world for the enlightenment of man's heart, the making straight before him all the ways of righteousness and truth, the implanting in his heart of fear for the judgements of God. A spirit of humility, patience, abundant compassion, perpetual goodness, insight, discrimination, a sense of the Divine Power that is based at once on an apprehension of God's works and a reliance on His plenteous mercy, a spirit of knowledge informing every plan of action, a zeal for righteous government, a hallowed mind in a controlled nature, abounding love for all who follow the truth, a self-respecting purity which abhors all the taint of filth, a modesty of behaviour coupled with a general prudence and an ability to hide within oneself the secrets of what one knows—these are the things that come to men in this world through communion with the spirit of truth. And the guerdon of all that walk in its ways is health and abundant well-being, with long life and fruition of seed along with eternal blessings and everlasting joy in the life everlasting, and a crown of glory and a robe of honour, amid light perpetual.

But to the spirit of perversity belong greed, remissness in right-doing, wickedness and falsehood, pride and presumption, deception and guile, cruelty and abundant insolence, shortness of temper and profusion of folly, arrogant passion, abominable acts in a spirit of lewdness, filthy ways in the thraldom of unchastity, a blasphemous tongue, blindness of eyes, dullness of ears, stiffness of neck and hardness of heart, to the end that a man walks entirely in ways of darkness and of evil cunning. The guerdon of all who walk in such ways is a multitude of afflictions at the hands of all the angels of destruction, everlasting perdition through the angry wrath of an avenging God, eternal horror and perpetual reproach, the disgrace of final annihilation in the Fire, darkness throughout the vicissitudes of life in every generation, doleful sorrow, bitter misfortune and darkling ruin—ending in extinction without remnant or survival.

It is to these things that all men are born, and it is to these that all the host of them are heirs throughout their generations. It is in these ways that men needs must walk and it is in these two divisions, according as a man inherits something of each, that all human acts are divided throughout all the ages of eternity. For God has appointed these two things to obtain in equal measure until the final age.

Between the two categories He has set an eternal enmity. Deeds of perversity are an abomination to Truth, while all the ways of Truth are an abomination to perversity; and there is a constant jealous rivalry between their two régimes, for they do not march in accord. Howbeit, God in His inscrutable wisdom has appointed a term for the existence of perversity, and when the time of Inquisition comes, He will destroy it for ever. Then Truth will emerge triumphant for the world, albeit now and until the time of the final judgement it will go on sullying itself in the ways of wickedness owing to the domination of perversity. Then, too, God will purge all the acts of man in the crucible of His truth, and refine for Himself all the fabric of man, destroying every spirit of perversity from within his flesh and cleansing him by the holy spirit from all the effects of wickedness. Like waters of purification He will sprinkle upon him the spirit of truth, to cleanse him of all the abominations of falsehood and of all pollution through the spirit of filth; to the end that, being made upright, men may have understanding of transcendental knowledge and of the lore of the sons of heaven, and that, being made blameless in their ways, they may be endowed with inner vision. For them has God chosen to be the partners of His eternal covenant, and theirs shall be all mortal glory. Perversity shall be no more, and all works of deceit shall be put to shame.

Thus far, the spirits of truth and perversity have been

struggling in the heart of man. Men have walked both in wisdom and in folly. If a man casts his portion with truth, he does righteously and hates perversity; if he casts it with perversity, he does wickedly and abominates truth. For God has apportioned them in equal measure until the final age, until "He makes all things new". He foreknows the effect of their works in every epoch of the world, and He has made men heirs to them that they might know good and evil. But [when the time] of Inquisition [comes], He will determine the fate of every living being in accordance with which of the [two spirits he has chosen to follow].

This is the rule for all the members of the community—that is, for such as have declared their readiness to turn away from all evil and to adhere to all that God in His good pleasure has commanded.

They are to keep apart from the company of the froward.

They are to belong to the community in both a doctrinal and an economic sense.

They are to abide by the decisions of the sons of Zadok, the same being priests that still keep the Covenant, and of the majority of the community that stand firm in it. It is by the vote of such that all matters doctrinal, economic and judicial are to be determined.

They are concertedly and in all their pursuits to practise truth, humility, righteousness, justice, charity and decency, with no-one walking in the stubbornness of his own heart or going astray after his heart or his eyes or his fallible human mind.

Furthermore, they are concertedly to remove the impurity of their human mould, and likewise all stiffneckedness.

They are to establish in Israel a solid basis of truth.

They are to unite in a bond indissoluble for ever.

They are to extend forgiveness to all among the priesthood that have freely enlisted in the cause of holiness, and to all among the laity that have done so in the cause of truth, and likewise to all that have associated themselves with them.

They are to make common cause both in the struggle and in the upshot of it.

They are to regard as felons all that transgress the law.

And this is the way in which all those ordinances are to be applied on a collective basis.

Everyone who is admitted to the formal organization of the community is to enter into a covenant in the presence of all fellow-volunteers in the cause and to commit himself by a binding oath to return with all his heart and soul to the commandments of the Law of Moses, as that Law is revealed to the sons of Zadok—that is, to the priests who still keep the Covenant and seek God's will—and to a majority of their co-covenanters who have volunteered together to adhere to the truth of God and to walk according to His pleasure.

He that so commits himself is to keep apart from all froward men that walk in the path of wickedness; for such men are not to be reckoned in the Covenant in as much as they have never sought nor studied God's ordinances in order to find out on what more arcane points they may guiltily have gone astray, while in regard to the things which stand patently revealed they have acted high-handedly. They have thus incurred God's angry judgement and caused Him to take vengeance upon them with all the curses threatened in the Covenant and to wreak great judgements upon them that they be finally destroyed without remnant.

No one is to go into water in order to attain the purity of holy men. For men cannot be purified except they repent their evil. God regards as impure all that transgress His word. No one is to have any association with such a man either in work or in goods, lest he incur the penalty of prosecution. Rather is he to keep away from such a man in every respect, for the Scripture says: "Keep away from every false thing" (Exodus 23. 7). No member of the community is to abide by the decision of such men in any matter of doctrine or law. He is not to eat or drink of anything that belongs to them nor to receive anything from them except for cash, even as it is written: "Desist from the man whose breath is in his nostrils, for as what is he reckoned?" (Isaias 2. 22). All that are not reckoned in the Covenant must be put aside, and likewise all that they possess. A holy man must not rely on works of vanity, and vanity is what all of them are that have not recognized God's Covenant.

All that spurn His word will God blast out of the world. All their actions are as filth before Him, and He regards all their possessions as unclean.

When a man enters the Covenant, minded to act in accordance with all the foregoing ordinances and formally to ally himself to the holy congregation, inquiry is to be made concerning his temper in human relations and his understanding and performance in matters of doctrine. This inquiry is to be conducted jointly by the priests who have undertaken concertedly to uphold God's Covenant and to supervise the execution of all the ordinances which He has commanded, and by a majority of the laity who have likewise undertaken concertedly to return to that Covenant. Every man is then to be registered in a particular rank, one after the other, by the standard of his understanding and performance. The object is that each person will be rendered subject to his superior. Their spiritual attitudes and their performance are to be reviewed, however, year by year, some being then promoted by virtue of their [improved] understanding and the integrity of their conduct, and others demoted for their waywardness.

When anyone has a charge against his neighbour, he is to prosecute it truthfully, humbly and humanely. He is not to speak to him angrily or querulously or arrogantly or in any wicked mood. He is not to bear hatred [towards him in the inner recesses] of his heart. When he has a charge against him, he is to proffer it then and there and not to render himself liable to penalty by nursing a grudge. Furthermore, no man is to bring a charge publicly against his neighbour except he prove it by witnesses.

This is the procedure which all members of the community are to follow in all dealings with one another, wherever they dwell.

Everyone is to obey his superior in rank in all matters of work or money. But all are to dine together, worship together and take counsel together.

Wherever there be ten men who have been formally enrolled in the community, one who is a priest is not to depart from them. When they sit in his presence, they are to take their places according to their respective ranks; and the same order is to obtain when they meet for common counsel.

When they set the table for a meal or prepare wine to drink, the priest is first to put forth his hand to invoke a blessing on the first portion of the bread or wine.

Similarly, wherever there be ten men who have been formally enrolled in the community, there is not to be absent from them one who can interpret the Law to them at any time of day or night, for the harmonious adjustment of their human relations.

The general members of the community are to keep awake for a third of all the nights of the year reading book(s) (or: the Book [of the Law]), studying the Law and worshipping together.

This is the rule covering public sessions.

The priests are to occupy the first place. The elders are to come second; and the rest of the people are to take their places according to their respective ranks. This order is to obtain alike when they seek a judicial ruling, when they meet for common counsel, or when any matter arises of general concern.

Everyone is to have an opportunity of rendering his opinion in the common council. No one, however, is to interrupt while his neighbour is speaking, or to speak until the latter has finished. Furthermore, no one is to speak in advance of his prescribed rank. Everyone is to speak in turn, as he is called upon.

In public sessions, no one is to speak on any subject that is not of concern to (or: is not to the liking of) the company as a whole. If the superintendent of the general membership or anyone who is not of the same rank as the person who happens to be raising a question for the consideration of the community, has something to say to the company, he is to stand up and declare: I have something to say to the company; and only if they so bid him, is he to speak.

If any man in Israel wish to be affiliated to the formal congregation of the community, the superintendent of the general membership is to examine him as to his intelligence and his actions and, if he then embark on a course of training, he is to have him enter into a covenant to return to the truth and turn away from all perversity. Then he is to appraise him of all the rules of the community.

Subsequently, when that man comes to present himself to the general membership, everyone is to be asked his opinion about him, and his admission to or rejection from the formal congregation of the community is to be determined by general vote.

No candidate, however, is to be admitted to the formal state of purity enjoyed by the general membership of the community until, at the completion of a full year, his spiritual attitude and his performance have been duly reviewed. Meanwhile he is to have no stake in the common funds.

After he has spent a full year in the midst of the community, the members are jointly to review his case, as to his understanding and performance in matters of doctrine. If it then be voted by the opinion of the priests and a majority of their co-covenanters to admit him to the sodality, they are to have him bring with him all his property and the tools of his profession. These are to be committed to the custody of the community's "minister of works". They are to be entered by that officer into an account, but he is not to disburse them for the general benefit.

Not until the completion of a second year among the members of the community is the candidate to be admitted to the common board. When, however, that second year has been completed, he is to be subjected to a further review by the general membership, and if then it be voted to admit him to the community, he is to be registered in the due order of rank which he is to occupy among his brethren in all matters pertaining to doctrine, judicial procedure, degree of purity and share in the common funds. Thenceforth his counsel and judgement are to be at the disposal of the community.

And these are the rules to be followed in the interpretation of the law regarding forms of speech.

If there be found in the community a man who consciously lies in the matter of (his) wealth, he is to be regarded as outside the state of purity entailed by membership, and he is to be mulcted of one fourth of his food ration for one year.

If a man answer his neighbour defiantly or speak brusquely

so as to undermine the composure of his fellow, and in so doing flout the orders of one who is registered as his superior, and if his hand act wickedly against him (?), he is to be mulcted for one year.

If a man, in speaking about anything, mention that Name which is honoured above all [names], or if, in a moment of sudden stress or for some other personal reason, he curse the precentor (?) [i.e. the man who reads the Book of the Law or leads worship], he is to be put out and never to return to formal membership in the community.

If a man speak in anger against one of the registered priests, he is to be mulcted for one year, placed in isolation and regarded as outside the state of purity entailed in membership of the community. If, however, he spoke unintentionally, he is to be mulcted only for six months.

If a man dissemble about what he really knows, he is to be mulcted for six months.

If a man defames his neighbour unjustly, and does so deliberately, he is to be mulcted for one year and regarded as "outside".

If a man speak with his neighbour in guile or consciously practise deceit upon him, he is to be mulcted for six months. If, however, he practises the deceit [unintentionally], he is to be mulcted only for three months.

If a man defraud the community, causing a deficit in its funds, he is to make good that deficit. If he lack means to do so, he is to be mulcted for sixty days.

If he harbour a grudge against his neighbour without legitimate cause, he is to be mulcted for six months [supralinear correction: "one year"]. The same is to apply also to anyone who takes personal revenge on his neighbour in any respect.

Anyone who indulges in indecent talk is to be mulcted for three months.

Anyone who interrupts his neighbour in a public session is to be mulcted for ten days.

Anyone who lies down and goes to sleep at a public session is to be mulcted for thirty days.

Anyone who leaves a public session gratuitously and without reason for as many as three times during one sitting is to be mulcted for ten days. If he be ordered to stay (?) and he still leave, he is to be mulcted for thirty days.

If, except he be under duress (?), a man walk naked before his neighbour, he shall be mulcted for six months.

If a man spit into the midst of a public session, he shall be mulcted for thirty days.

If a man bring out his hand from under his cloak, and so expose himself that his private parts become visible, he shall be mulcted for thirty days.

If a man indulge in raucous, inane laughter, he shall be mulcted for thirty days.

If a man put forth his left hand to gesticulate with it in conversation, he shall be mulcted for ten days.

If a man slander his neighbour, he shall be regarded as outside the communal state of purity for one year, and he shall also be mulcted. But if he slander the entire group, he is to be expelled and never to return.

If a man complain against the whole basis of the community, he is to be expelled irrevocably.

If he complain against his neighbour without legitimate cause, he is to be mulcted for six months.

If a man's spirit waver so far from the basis of the community that he betray the truth and walk in the stubbornness of his own heart, but if he subsequently repent, he shall be mulcted for two years. During the first, he shall be regarded as outside the communal state of purity altogether. During the second, he shall be excluded only from the common board and occupy a place behind all the other members. At the completion of the two years, the membership in general shall hold an inquiry about him. If it then be decided to readmit him, he shall again be registered with duly assigned rank, and thereafter he too shall be called upon to render his opinion in deliberations concerning the rules.

If a man has been a formal member of the community for a full ten years, but then, through a spiritual relapse, betray the principles of the community and quit the general body in order to walk in the stubbornness of his own heart, he is never to return to formal membership in the community. No member of the community is to associate with him either by recognizing him as of the same state of purity or by sharing property with him. Any of the members who does so shall be liable to the same sentence: he too shall be expelled.

What follows this repeats in a more concise form the aim of the community and makes more precise the condition for the admission and formation of the members; it contains the following somewhat curious passage.

When these men have undergone, with blamelessness of conduct, a two-year preparation in the fundamentals of the community, they shall be segregated as specially sacred among the formal members of the community. Any knowledge which the expositor of the law may possess but which may have to remain arcane to the ordinary layman, he shall not keep hidden from them; for in their case there need be no fear that it might induce apostasy.

The punishment of those who defect is then laid down in great detail.

Then comes the positive and spiritual part; the strict rule must blossom forth and produce fruits of justice and wisdom.

These are the ordinances for the conduct of any man that seeks after inner vision, in regard alike to human relations, the regulation of affairs on specific occasions, and the balanced appraisal of his fellow men, to the end that he may perform at all times the will of God which has been revealed as pertinent to this or that occasion; that he may at all times accommodate (abstract) theory to (concrete) circumstance; and that he may come to make the proper distinctions and evaluate (both the clergy), the sons of Zadok and the elect of any specific epoch by the standard of their spiritual attitudes, and appraise them by that criterion, thus conforming to the will of God, as He has commanded.

Everyone is to be judged by the standard of his spirituality. Intercourse with him is to be determined by the purity of his deeds, and consort with him by the degree of his intelligence. This alone is to determine the degree to which a man is to be loved or hated.

No one is to engage in discussion or disputation with men of ill repute; and in the company of froward men everyone is to abstain from talk about the meaning of the Law [*Torah*].

With those, however, that have chosen the right path everyone is indeed to discuss matters pertaining to the apprehension of God's truth and of His righteous judgements. The purpose of such discussions is to guide the minds of the members of the community, to give them insight into God's inscrutable wonders and truth, and to bring them to walk blamelessly each with his neighbour in harmony with all that has been revealed to them. For this is the time when "the way is being prepared in the wilderness", and it behooves them to understand all that is happening. It is also the time when they must needs keep apart from all other men and not turn aside from the way through any form of perversity.

And these are the regulations of conduct for every man that would seek the inner vision in these times, touching what he is to love and what he is to hate.

He is to bear unremitting hatred towards all men of ill repute, and to be minded to keep in seclusion from them. He is to leave it to them to pursue wealth and mercenary gain, like servants at the mercy of their masters or wretches truckling to a despot.

He is to be zealous to carry out every ordinance punctiliously, against the Day of Requital.

In all his emprises and in all things over which he has control he is to act in a manner acceptable to God, in accordance with what God has commanded.

He is to accept willingly whatever befalls him and to take pleasure in nothing but the will of God.

He is to make [all] the words of his mouth acceptable, and not to lust after anything that God has not commanded.

He is to watch ever for the judgement of God, and [in every vicissitude of his existence] he is to bless his Maker. Whatever befalls, he is to [recount God's glory] and to bless Him [with "the oblation of] the lips".

The Hymn of the Initiants

When daylight begins its rule,
when it reaches its turning-point,
and when it again withdraws to its appointed abode;

When the watches of darkness begin,
when God opens the storehouse thereof,
when He sets that darkness against the light,
when it reaches its turning-point,
and when it again withdraws in face of the light;

When sun and moon shine forth from the holy Height,
and when they again withdraw to the glorious Abode;

When the formal seasons come on the days of new moon,
when they reach their turning-points,
and when they yield place to one another,
as each comes round anew;

When the natural seasons come, at whatever time may be;
when, too, the months begin;
on their feasts and on holy days,
as they come in order due,
each as a memorial in its season—

I shall hold it as one of the laws
engraven of old on the tablets
to render to God as my tribute
—the blessings of my lips.

When the (natural) years begin;
at the turning-points of their seasons,
and when each completes its term
on its natural day,
yielding each to each—
reaping-time to summer,
sowing-time to verdure;
In the (formal) years of weeks,
in the several seasons thereof,
and when, at the jubilee,
the series of weeks begins—

I shall hold it as one of the laws
engraven of old on the tablets
to offer to God as my fruits—
the praises of my tongue,
and to cull for Him as my tithe
—the skilled music of my lips.

With the coming of day and night
I shall come ever anew
into God's covenant;
and when evening and morning depart,
shall observe how He sets their bounds.

Only where God sets bounds
—the unchangeable bounds of His Law—
will I too set my domain.

I shall hold it as one of the laws
engraven of old on the tablets
to face my sin and transgression
and avouch the justice of God.
I shall say unto God:
"Thou, for me, art the Right!"
and unto the Most High:
"For me Thou art cause of all good!"

Fountain of all knowledge,
Spring of holiness,
Zenith of all glory,
Might omnipotent,
Beauty that never fades,
I will choose the path He shows me,
and be content with His judgements.

Whenever I first put forth my hand or foot,
I will bless His name;
when first I go or come,
when I sit and when I rise,
when I lie down on my couch,
I will sing unto Him.

At the common board,
or ever I raise my hand
to enjoy the rich fruits of the earth,
with that which flows from my lips
I will bless Him as with an oblation.

At the onset of fear and alarm,
or when trouble and stress are at hand,
I will bless Him with special thanksgiving
and must meditate upon His power,
and rely on His mercies alway,
and come thereby to know
that in His hand lies the judgement of all living,
and that all His works are truth.

Whenever distress breaks out,
I still will praise Him;
and when His salvation comes,
join the chorus of praise.

I will heap no evil on any,
but pursue all men with good,
knowing that only with God
lies the judgement of all living,
and He it is will award
each man his deserts.

I will not be envious
of the profit of wickedness;
for wealth unrighteously gotten my soul shall not lust.

I will not engage in strife
with reprobate men,
forestalling the Day of Requital.

I will not turn back my wrath
from froward men,
nor rest content until justice be affirmed.

I will harbour no angry grudge
against those that indeed repent,
but neither will I show compassion
to any that turn from the way.

I will not console the smitten
until they amend their course.

I will cherish no baseness in my heart,
nor shall there be heard in my mouth
coarseness or wanton deceit;
neither shall there be found upon my lips
deception and lies.

The fruit of holiness shall be on my tongue,
and no heathen filth be found thereon.
I will open my mouth with thanksgiving,
and my tongue shall ever relate
the bounteousness of God
and the perfidy of men
until men's transgressions be ended.

Empty words will I banish from my lips;
filth and perverseness from my mind.
I will shelter knowledge with sound counsel,
and protect [it] with shrewdness of mind.
I will [set] a sober limit
to all defending of faith
and exacting of justice by force.
I will bound God's righteousness
by the measuring-line of occasion.
[I will temper] justice [with mercy],
will show kindness to men downtrodden,
bring firmness to fearful hearts,
discernment to spirits that stray,
enlighten the bowed with sound doctrine,
reply to the proud with meekness,
with humility answer the base
—men rich in worldly goods,

who point the finger of scorn
and utter iniquitous thoughts.

To God I commit my cause.
It is His to perfect my way,
His to make straight my heart.
He, in His charity,
will wipe away my transgression.

For He from the Wellspring of Knowledge
has made His light to burst forth,
and mine eye has gazed on His wonders;
and the light that is in my heart
has pierced the deep things of existence.

He is ever the stay of my right hand.
The path beneath my feet
is set on a mighty rock
unshaken before all things.

For that rock beneath my feet
is the truth of God,
and His power is the stay of my right hand;
from the fount of His charity
my vindication goes forth.

Blessed art Thou, O my God,
Who hast opened the heart of Thy servant unto knowledge.
Direct all his works in righteousness,
and vouchsafe unto the son of Thine handmaid
the favour which Thou hast assured to all the mortal elect,
to stand in Thy presence for ever.
For apart from Thee no man's way can be perfect,
and without Thy will is nothing wrought.

Thou it is that hath taught all knowledge,
and all things exist by Thy will;
and there is none beside Thee
to controvert Thy plan;

none to understand all Thy holy thought,
none to gaze into the depths of Thy secrets,
none to perceive all Thy wonders and the might of Thy power.

Who can compass the sum of Thy glory?
and what is mere mortal man
amid Thy wondrous works?
And what the child of woman
to sit in Thy presence?
For, behold, he is kneaded of dust,
and his portion is the food of worms.
He is but a moulded shape,
a thing nipped out of the clay,
whose attachment is but to the dust.
What can such clay reply,
or that which is moulded by hand?
What thought can it comprehend?

What is noticeable here is the desire to be apart from the world, a notion very different from that of the "chosen people" which had governed the thought and the history of the Jews. In the Bible, it is the whole people that belongs to the Lord, and his teaching is addressed to all, as is the preaching of the prophets. But now there is a separation of the good from the wicked within the Jewish people itself. It is no longer a matter of Yahweh's choice but of the choice of man himself: the postulant acts of his own will, and is accepted or rejected by other men. The common Hellenistic idea of the sect, a group "cut off", had found its way into the minds even of the purest of the pure. And we can notice with interest another pagan notion that had found its way in: the Lord is called "God of knowledge", which is a Platonist or Gnostic expression, and certainly not biblical. It shows clearly, as does the doctrine of the "two spirits", the close relationship with Mazdaean dualism. True, this is not, as it was for the Persians, belief in a god of good and a god of evil; but there is no mention anywhere in the Old Testament of these two spirits dividing the world between them.

We may also notice the mention of a secret teaching, reserved to the just alone; this is opposed to the constant tradition of Holy Scripture, but very much in the spirit of the Hellenistic sects.

All the same, the Essenes were very different. They had no faith in the military tactics of the followers of the Machabees; they had none in the political machinations in which the Pharisees wasted their strength; they saw in the events of their times sure signs announcing the Day of the Lord and the coming of the Messias. So they withdrew from the sinful world, sure that the Lord had set them apart from all time to be the last faithful remnant. Their only ambition was to preserve as rigorously as they could the letter and the spirit of the Law. We can see from the ruins of the monastery at Qumran that it was a building designed specially for a strictly ritualistic life.

Together with the rule belonging to the community of Qumran there was discovered a text that had already been known for sixty years or more: the Zadokite Document. It is more historical, less divorced from its political and human context than the rule of the community; but it had remained a puzzling and obscure text, deprived as it was of any background. Now, at the same time as it sheds a good deal of light on the other texts discovered by reason of the chronological relations it makes it possible to establish, it has taken its own place in a context in which it can be more easily understood. It is as it were another rule for the community, but belonging to another period in the history of the Essenes.

The excavations at Qumran have shown that it was built about 110 B.C. and destroyed between A.D. 68 and 70, but that it was not continually occupied, there being a gap when the site was abandoned, from about 40 B.C. to the beginning of our era. Now the Zadokite Document does not refer to a community life in the desert but to small communities, perhaps, scattered among ordinary society. So some have thought that it is, as it were, an outlying witness to this exodus of the dwellers at Qumràn at a time when a measure of peace had returned to Israel. But there are important differences: the faithful to whom the Zadokite Document is addressed accept as right sacrifices offered in the temple at Jerusalem, and it is clear that in several places they could be married, which was most likely impossible at Qumran (though some skeletons of women and children have been found in the cemetery). Are we dealing with the same sect, at a time other than that at which Qumran was abandoned for forty years (which would imply a schism among the Essenes), or with a kind of "third order" for those who, bound by family responsibilities, could not retreat into the desert? The question cannot at present be answered.

Since the rule of the Zadokite community is very similar, with the differences just mentioned, to that of Qumran, and in any case shares the same spirit, I shall only quote the historical passages from the Document.

Again and again we are told of the apostasy of Israel, but such is the apocalyptic style that we cannot fit the story into a firm historical framework. But what we know of the indescribable confusion of religious and political affairs in Israel about the time of the beginning of our era leaves us in little doubt about the times to which the Document refers.

And here we meet the enigmatic figure of the so-called "teacher of righteousness", the founder of the sect. Although this holy personage has not been identified, it seems clear that he can no longer be thought of as a Messias, to be opposed to Christ. True, the Essenes were awaiting the coming of the Messias, and if they led a life apart in the desert it was so as to be able to prepare the better for his future advent. But their founder was a prophet of these latter times, sent, as was said of John the Baptist, to "prepare the way of the Lord"; but the Messias, son of David, was still to come.

Israel's apostasy:

Meanwhile, however, Belial will be rampant in Israel, even as God has said through the prophet Isaiah, the son of Amoz: "Terror and the pit and the trap shall be upon thee, O inhabitant of the land!" (24. 17). The reference is to those three snares, viz., (a) whoredom, (b) lucre, and (c) desecration, concerning which Levi the son of Jacob said that by making them look like three kinds of righteousness Belial ensnares Israel in them. He who escapes the one gets caught in the other, and he who escapes the other gets caught in the third.

Such men may be described as "builders of a rickety wall" Ezech. 13. 10), or as persons that have "walked after filth" (Hos. 5. 11). The "filth" in question is the babbling preacher of whom God said, "Babble-babble shall they preach" (Micah 2. 6); while the fact that *two* words [viz., "pit" and "trap"] are used to describe the net in which they will be caught alludes to the whorish practice of taking *two* wives at the same time, the true basis of nature being the pairing of one male with one female, even as it is said (of Adam and Eve), "A male and a female created He them" (Gen. 1. 27), and of those that went into the ark, "In pairs they entered" (Gen. 7. 9). Similarly, too, it is said concerning a prince: "He shall not take more than one wife" (Deut. 17. 17).

David, however, had never read the Book of Law, for it was sealed up in the ark and remained unopened in Israel from the day when Eleazar and Joshua and the Elders were gathered to their rest. The people worshipped Ashtoreth, while the ark remained hidden and unopened until indeed a Zadokite entered into office [in the person of Hilkiah the priest]. Accordingly, David's actions were not punished, save the spilling of the blood of Uriah, but God remitted the penalty for them.

Such persons commit [desecration] in as much as they lie with women in their periods and do not put them aside, as enjoined in the Law. Moreover, they marry the daughters of their brothers and sisters, whereas Moses has said: "Thou shalt not enter into intimate relations with the sister of thy mother; she is thy mother's kin" (cf. Lev. 18. 13). (The laws of forbidden degrees are written, to be sure, with reference to males, but they hold good equally for females. A niece, for instance, who indulges in carnal intercourse with her paternal uncle is equally to be regarded as his kin.)

Furthermore, such men have desecrated the holy spirit within them, and with mocking tongue have opened their mouths against the statutes of God's Covenant, declaring, "They have no foundation". They have spoken disgracefully about them.

All such men may be described as persons that "kindle a fire and set firebrands alight" (Isaias 50. 11). Of them it may be said that "their webs are spiders' webs and their eggs basilisks' eggs" (Isaias 59. 5). None that have contact with them shall go unscathed; the more one does so, the more guilty he becomes—unless, of course, he does so under compulsion.

Throughout antiquity, however, God has always taken note of the deeds of such men, and His anger has always been kindled against their acts. Always, in fact, they have proved to be "a witless folk" (Isaias 27. 11), a nation void of sense (Deut. 32. 28) in that they lacked discernment.

When, in antiquity, Israel was first delivered, Moses and Aaron still continued in their charge, through the help of the Angel of Lights, even though Belial in his cunning had set up James and his brother in opposition to them.

The origins of the sect:

Now listen, all right-minded men, and take note how God acts: He has a feud with all flesh and exacts satisfaction from all who spurn him.

Whenever Israel broke faith and renounced Him, He hid His face both from it and from His sanctuary and consigned them to the sword. But whenever He called to mind the Covenant which He had made with their forebears, He spared them a remnant and did not consign them to utter extinction.

So, in the Era of Anger, that era of the three hundred and ninety years, when He delivered them into the hand of Nebuchadnezzar, king of Babylon, He took care of them and brought to blossom alike out of the priesthood and out of the laity that root which had been planted of old, allowing it once more to possess the land and to grow fat in the richness of its soil. Then they realized their iniquity and knew that they had been at fault. For twenty years, however, they remained like blind men groping their way, until at last God took note of their deeds, how that they were seeking Him sincerely, and He raised up for them one who would teach the Law correctly (usually rendered: "Teacher of Righteousness"), to guide them in the way of His heart and to demonstrate to future ages what He does to a generation that incurs His anger, that is, to the congregation of those that betray Him and turn aside from His way.

The period in question was that whereof it is written, "Like a stubborn heifer, Israel was stubborn" (Hos. 4. 16). It was a time when a certain scoffer arose to distil upon Israel the waters deceptive and to lead them astray in a trackless waste, bringing low whatsoever had once been high, diverting them from the proper paths and removing the landmarks which their forebears had set up, to the end that through his efforts those curses cleaved to them which had been prescribed when the Covenant was concluded, and they were delivered to the sword. Thus was avenged the breach of the Covenant which they had committed in seeking smooth things and in preferring delusion and in being constantly on the watch to breach the faith and in choosing to walk proudly and in justifying the wicked and condemning the righteous, and in abrogating the Covenant and annulling the pact, and in assailing the life of the righteous and abhorring all whose conduct was blameless, and in pursuing them with the sword, and in raising a general clamour against them. God then grew angry with their horde and utterly destroyed all their throng and treated all their works as an abominable thing unclean.

Howbeit, with the rest of them, that is, with those that held fast to His commandments, God ever made good His everlasting Covenant with Israel, revealing to them the hidden things concerning which Israel in general had gone astray—even His holy sabbaths and His glorious festivals, His righteous ordinances, the ways of His truth and the purposes of His will, "the which, if a man do, he shall live" (Lev. 18. 5). He opened for them a well with water abounding, which they might dig. But them that spurned those waters He did not permit to live. And though they kept sullying themselves with human transgression and with filthy ways, and kept saying, " 'Tis our own concern", yet did God with His mysterious power shrive their iniquity and forgive their transgression and build for them in Israel a firmly established House the like of which has not existed from ancient times until this day.

They that hold fast unto Him are destined for life eternal, and theirs is all mortal glory, even as God has sworn unto them by the hand of the prophet Ezekiel, saying: "The priests and the levites and the sons of Zadok that kept the charge of My sanctuary when the children of Israel went astray from Me, these it is that shall offer unto Me the fat and the blood" (Ezech. 44. 15). By "priests" is meant those in Israel that repented and departed from the land of Judah. [By "levites"] is meant those that associated themselves with them. By "sons of Zadok" is meant those elect of Israel that have been designated by name and that shall go on functioning in these last days. Behold, their names have been specified, the families into which they are to be born, the epochs in which they are to function, the full tale of their tribulations, the length of their sojourn in exile and the precise nature of their deeds.

These were the "holy men" of former times—the men whose sins God pardoned, who knew right for right and wrong for wrong. But all who up to the present time have succeeded them in carrying out explicitly the Law from which those ancients drew their lessons, them too will God forgive, in accordance with the Covenant, which He made with those ancients to forgive their iniquities. And when the present era is completed, there will be no more express affiliation with the house of Judah; every man will "mount guard" for himself. "The fence will be rebuilt, and the bounds be far-flung" (cf. Micah 7. 11).

Beyond any doubt, the reaction of the Essenes is a very important manifestation of the resistance of Israel to the invaders. But the Essenes did not defend themselves and the spirit of Israel only by cultivating the interior life and their own sanctity, and placing all their hope in the Lord. In the texts we have quoted it can be seen that they entertained a most lively hatred against their enemies, and even made it almost a requirement of membership. There would surely be nothing surprising in that hatred bursting out into violence, even war, if the chance occurred. "The War of the Sons of Light and the Sons of Darkness", a text unknown before, which is a curious mixture of apocalypse and strategy, gives us some idea of the way in which the "children of light" thought they might carry on the fight against the impious if the chance occurred.

> The trumpets shall keep sounding for the slingers until they have hurled a full seven times. Then the priests shall blow the recall for them, and they shall return to the first line to take their stand in their assigned position. Thereupon the priests shall sound a blast on the trumpets of assembly, and the squadron of infantry shall go forth from the gaps and take up position between the lines, and on their flanks shall be horsemen to the right and to the left. The priests shall then sound upon the trumpets a quavering (?) blast for the drawing up of the line of battle. The columns shall disperse to their several ranks, each to his assigned position. And when they have taken up position in three lines, the priests shall sound a second blast—a low, subdued note for advance to the enemy line. Thereupon they are to grasp their weapons. Then the priests are to sound blasts on the six trumpets used for rousing to the slaughter—a sharp insistent note for directing the battle. And the levites and all the people with rams' horns are to sound a single blast—a great warlike trump to melt the heart of the enemy. At the sound of that blast, the war-darts are to issue forth to fell the slain. Then they are to accelerate the notes on the rams' horns, and the priests are to blow on the trumpets a sharp insistent sound to direct the wings of the battle, until they have hurled their darts into the enemy line seven times.

Thereupon the priests are to sound upon the trumpets the signal of recall—a low, quavering (?) subdued note.

In such fashion are the priests to blow the signals for the three squadrons. And when the first squadron begins to hurl its darts, the [priests] are to blow [ ] [on the trump]et a great blast to direct the bat[tle] [ ]; the priests are to sound a blast for them on the trumpets [ ] their assigned position in the ranks [ ], and [ ] shall take up position.

When they come up from gathering in the fallen and return to the camps, they shall all of them sing the hymn of return. Next morning, they shall launder their garments and wash themselves clean of the blood of the guilty corpses and return to their assigned places where the line was drawn up before the slain of the enemy fell. And there they shall all of them bless the God of Israel and extol His name together in joy and take up word and say:

Blessed be the God of Israel
Who keeps the loyalty of His covenant
and constantly evinces salvation
to the people whom He redeemed.
He has summoned those that were stumbling [ ],
but has gathered the horde of the heathen for extermination without survival,
exalting the melting heart by [His] justice,
opening the mouth of the dumb for joyful song,
endowing with strength hands that were slack,
teaching them arts of war;
giving firm stance to tottering knees
and vigour to the shoulders of the bowed;
and [ ] to the lowly spirits;
firmness to the melting heart,
and [ ] to those whose way is blameless.
All wicked nations are come to an end
and all their heroes have no standing.
But we—[Thou hast granted us] a remnant;
[therefore we will bless] Thy name.
O God of mercies,
Who keepest the covenant sworn unto our fathers,

and Who, through all our generations,
hast wondrously shown forth Thy mercies unto our remnant,
[Thou hast caused us to prevail] against the dominion of Belial
that, for all his covert hostility,
he has not thrust us away from Thy covenant.
Thou hast preserved the life
of [the people] whom Thou didst redeem;
hast upholden the falling by Thy strength,
and cut down all the proud of stature.
Their warriors have none to deliver them;
their fleet men have no escape;
their honoured men Thou turnest to contempt;
and every creature of vanity [Thou reducest to nau]ght.
But we—we are Thy holy people;
for Thy holy works we will praise Thy name,
and for Thy deeds of power we will extol [Thy] [ ],
at all the stated times, and at all the foreordained moments of nature:
at the coming of day and night,
and the outgoing of evening and morning;
for great is [ ] of Thy [ ]
and Thy mysterious wonders in the heights.
For Thou raisest up unto Thee out of the dust,
and castest down from the angels.

This holy war is begun with this magnificent song by the high priest:

Arise, O warrior!
Take thy captives, thou man of glory;
and reap thy spoil, O valiant!
Set thy hand upon the neck of thy foemen,
and thy foot upon the mounds of the slain.
Smite the nations that assail thee,
and let thy sword devour guilty flesh.
Fill thy land with glory
and thine inheritance with blessing.
Be a multitude of possessions in thy fields,
silver and gold and precious stones in thy palaces.

Zion, rejoice exceedingly,
and shine forth, O Jerusalem, with songs of joy,
and let all the cities of Judah exult!
Let thy gates be continually open,
that the wealth of the nations may be brought unto thee;
and let their kings minister unto thee,
and all that oppressed thee make obeisance to thee,
and lick the dust of thy feet!
O daughter of my people,
ring out your songs of joy!
Put on your finery,
step forth [ ]
[ ] Israel, to rule for evermore!
[ ] the warriors, O Jerusalem!
Be exalted, O Lord, above the heavens!

Surely what we have found at Qumran is a living illustration of all the tendencies that we have seen scattered throughout the apocrypha: the exaltation of Israel, the fanatical hope that God would not abandon his people, the waiting for deliverance and for the Messias, the infiltration of some Hellenistic ideas, and the search for the interior life.

As the Essenes thought, the time of the New Covenant had come.

CONCLUSION

Now that we have come to the end of our rapid survey of the apocryphal literature of the Old Testament, what conclusions can we draw? How do the apocryphal books differ, essentially, from those of the Old Testament itself?

Whatever their different aims, their different forms, and their differences of spirit, all have one feature in common: all, in their different ways, unwittingly strive to accommodate the message of the Scriptures to a too human viewpoint. There is a tendency towards syncretism, in the attempt to accommodate the first chapters of Genesis to a civilization imbued with pagan cosmologies. There is a tendency towards conformism, in the attempt to make the patriarchs into something like the mythological heroes. And there was the temptation, more subtle still, to withdraw into a rigid separatism, when men felt the need to harden themselves against the world, as if God needed to be defended by men.

When the synagogue and the Church excluded them from the canon of the Scriptures, they were merely applying to their writers the words Job spoke to his friends:

> First I would prove you what you are, unskilful plasterers all of you, that follow false rules of your craft. Would you but hold your tongues once for all! It were your best wisdom. Listen while I refute you; mark well what are my pleadings. Do you think God stands in need of your shifts, your lying advocacy? Are you God's hired partisans, resolved to acquit him? Why then, beware of his own infallible scrutiny; think you he will be blinded, as men are blinded, by your sophistries? Nay, he himself will be the first to blame you for wrongful attachment to his cause; your turn, then, to fear every movement of his, to cower before his terrors! (Job 13. 4–11).

It is a severe judgement, as was that of St Jerome on the apocrypha, but it shows a righteous respect for the word of God.

Yet perhaps our survey of these works has not been useless. It is impossible to view without emotion the beginnings of those persecutions, so similar throughout the ages, which have ceaselessly afflicted this people, come from the beginning of time, and from the beginning of time so unshakably loyal to their faith.

And these works will perhaps help us to understand better some passages of the Gospels: the resentment of the Pharisees against a Messias who told an oppressed people to pay their taxes to Caesar; and the opposition to the message of the Beatitudes from a people fanatically brave and hard-headed; and their handing over to the Romans of this Galilaean agitator with his contempt for the sabbath, in the hope that they themselves, the faithful, might thus gain some respite for the practice of the religious life.

We can better understand also the real preparation that the Essenes, with their search for perfection and their break away from certain forms of traditional Judaism, made for the Gospel message, for a "New Covenant" open to all men.

SELECT BIBLIOGRAPHY

In this series: DANIEL-ROPS: *What is the Bible?* DU BUIT, F., O.P.: *Biblical Archaeology*; GÉLIN, Albert: *The Religion of Israel*; HERVIEUX, Jacques: *The New Testament Apocrypha*; RÉGAMEY, P.-R., O.P.: *What is an Angel?* STEINMANN, Jean: *Biblical Criticism.*

ALLEGRO, J. M.: *The Dead Sea Scrolls*, Harmondsworth and Baltimore, Penguin Books, 1956.

BURROWS, Millar: *The Dead Sea Scrolls*, London, Secker and Warburg, and New York, Viking Press, 1955.

CHARLES, R. H.: *The Apocrypha and Pseudepigrapha of the Old Testament in English*, London and New York, Oxford Univ. Press, 1913; *Religious Development between the Old and the New Testament*, London and New York, Oxford Univ. Press, 1914.

DUPONT-SOMMER, A.: *The Jewish Sect of the Qumran and the Essenes*, New York, Macmillan, 1954.

GASTER, T. H.: *The Scriptures of the Dead Sea Sect in English Translation*, London, Secker and Warburg, and New York, Doubleday, 1957.

PFEIFFER, C. F.: *Between the Testaments*, Grand Rapids, Mich., Baker Books, 1959.

RAWLEY, H. H.: *The Zadokite Fragment and the Dead Sea Scrolls*, London and New York, Oxford Univ. Press, 1952.

SUTCLIFFE, E., S.J.: *The Monks of Qumran*, London, Burns and Oates, and Westminster, Md, Newman Press, 1960.

TORREY, C. C.: *The Apocryphal Literature*, New Haven, Conn., Yale Univ. Press, 1945.

The Twentieth Century Encyclopedia of Catholicism

The number of each volume indicates its place in the over-all series and not the order of publication.

PART ONE: KNOWLEDGE AND FAITH

1. What Does Man Know?
2. Is Theology a Science?
3. The Meaning of Tradition
4. What is Dogma?
5. Do Dogmas Change?
6. What is Faith?
7. God's Word to Man
8. Myth or Mystery?
9. What is a Miracle?
10. Is There a Christian Philosophy?
11. The Origins of Christian Philosophy
12. Medieval Christian Philosophy
13. The Basis of Belief
14. Christianity and Science
15. The God of Reason

PART TWO: THE BASIC TRUTHS

16. The Worship of God
17. What is the Trinity?
18. The Holy Spirit
19. The Creation
20. The Problem of Evil
21. Who is the Devil?
22. Freedom and Providence
23. The Theology of Grace
24. What is the Incarnation?
25. What is Redemption?
26. The Communion of Saints
27. Faith, Hope and Charity
28. Life After Death

Titles are subject to change.